DOMINIQUE
MOCEANU

Also by Krista Quiner

Shannon Miller: America's Most Decorated Gymnast

Kim Zmeskal: Determination to Win

DOMINIQUE MOCEANU
A GYMNASTICS SENSATION

A Biography by Krista Quiner

THE BRADFORD BOOK COMPANY
East Hanover, New Jersey

Printed in the United States of America
First Edition
10 9 8 7 6 5 4 3 2

Photo Credits:
All photographs and artwork were produced by Steve Lange, unless otherwise noted.

Library of Congress Cataloging-in-Publication Data

Quiner, Krista, 1970-
    Dominique Moceanu : A gymnastics sensation :
  a biography / by Krista Quiner. — 1st ed.
      p. cm.
  Includes bibliographical references (p. 186).
    1. Moceanu, Dominique, 1981- 2. Gymnasts—United
  States—Biography. I. Title.
GV460.2.M63Q55 1997
796.44'092—dc20
[B]   96-41525
                                     CIP

ISBN: 0-9643460-3-6

*For my grandparents, Earl and Velma Bailey
and Paul and Frances McKenzie,
who have encouraged me more than they know*

*To Dominique Moceanu,
who brings joy to the sport she loves*

ACKNOWLEDGMENTS

———•◦●●◦•———

Many thanks to Barry Quiner, my husband, whose name should also appear on the cover; Cara Bailey, my sister, whose enthusiasm and editing were invaluable; and Steve Lange, who takes some of the finest shots in gymnastics. Thanks also to the Karolyi's athletes Kim Zmeskal, Kerri Strug, Hilary Grivich, Betty Okino, Monica Flammer, and Jennie Thompson; the LaFleur's gymnasts Emily Spychala, Becky Waters, Shelly Cavaliere, Becky Wildgen, and Reneé Barnett; the coaches Jeff and Julie LaFleur, Beth Hair, Toni Rand, Geza Pozsar, James Holmes, John Geddert, and Artur Akopyan; and the parents and teachers Jean Pallardy, Jan Spychala, and Deanna Graves, for sharing their interesting stories and thoughts with me. And personal thanks to Paul Quiner for lending his expertise.

CONTENTS

Chapter 1

Destined from Birth

The gym is empty except for three gymnasts and two coaches. One of the athletes is tall and elegant; another is quick and powerful. The third is captivating. She commands the coaches' attention. Bubbly and charming, she dances and tumbles as though frolicking on a playground. She seems to have such fun, it is hard to believe she is working to become the best gymnast in the world.

In a few weeks she will be put to the test. She has practiced her whole life for what will amount to only minutes of performing. She has practiced to ensure she can handle any hardship on that day. She knows what it is like to have the flu and push herself through a beam routine feeling dizzy and out of balance. She has learned how to complete an entire floor routine despite a

1

throbbing heel injury or a shooting pain in her shin. She has pushed herself through one more vault when she thought her wrists would snap in half if she tried again. She has gone through her bar set with hands that were bleeding and sore.

She will be ready for the test when it comes. For now, it is quiet and safe in the gym. No television cameras zooming in for that up-close-and-personal shot. No reporters thrusting microphones in her face. No autograph seekers. No screaming fans. Nothing to distract her from the next routine.

She twirls around the bar, flips gracefully, lands flawlessly. She glances at her coach, who motions a slight correction. She nods and wipes more chalk on her callused hands. To the untrained eye her movements seem perfect, but she knows there are always improvements to be made. Her coach taught her that.

She jumps back on the apparatus and repeats the maneuver. The coach grunts his approval. A few more tries, then it is time to work on something else. She is always working. Always striving. Always improving.

This is elite gymnastics. The pressure can be suffocating. Perfection is the elusive goal. The mood is serious.

But it doesn't seem so serious the way this bundle of energy in a leotard cavorts about. She romps on each apparatus as if it's a game, whether dancing on the floor, skipping down the beam, flying around the bars, or soaring above the vault. Not only does she make it look easy, she makes it look *fun*. And for a sport beset by bad publicity of late—stories of lost childhoods, painful injuries, eating disorders, unhealthy attitudes, harmful parental pressures, and egomaniacal coaches—her indomitable spirit and positive attitude have been a much-needed breath of fresh air.

She is fourteen-year-old Dominique Moceanu, and a life in gymnastics is the only life she knows. She has been training since she was three and cannot remember life without her sport.

She is doing what she is supposed to be doing, what has been planned for her from birth. But most importantly, she is doing what she loves, what she has always wanted to do.

She is becoming one of the top gymnasts in the world, a true gymnastics sensation.

Dominique Helena Moceanu (pronounced mo-chee-AH-new) was born in Hollywood, California, on September 30, 1981—a few months after legendary gymnastics coach Bela Karolyi defected from Romania to the United States. Like their country-man, Dominique's parents had fled Romania in search of a better life.

In 1979, twenty-four-year-old Dimitry Moceanu applied for a passport—a document not easy to obtain in communist Romania. When government officials asked him to pick it up, his father urged him not to go, insisting that it was a trap and that he would be arrested. Dimitry dismissed his father's warning and obtained a tourist visa to Austria without incident. Believing his future lay in America, he left behind his eighteen-year-old girl-friend, Camelia, and his job as manager of a duty-free store to begin a journey to the land of opportunity.

Once in Austria, Dimitry sought political asylum in the United States. A church in Chicago agreed to sponsor him and brought him to the city. When Dimitry arrived, he spoke virtually no English, had very little money, and did not know a soul. The church found him a place to stay, and within days he secured a job at a Greek restaurant called Aphrodite's. He worked there for a few months, but when sweetheart Camelia needed him, he left promptly.

Attempting to reach her beau, Camelia had secured a passport, left Romania, and made her way as far as Greece. Dimitry traversed the Atlantic to be reunited with her after being apart for almost a year. The two stayed in Greece long enough to get married, honeymoon, and conceive their first child.

The newlyweds flew to New York City in February 1981. Dimitry's brother, Costa, who had also defected to the United States, invited them to join him in southern California. He knew of a job running a school cafeteria that suited Dimitry since he had experience in the food industry. Dimitry and Camelia accepted Costa's offer and scrounged up enough money for two bus tickets to Los Angeles.

It was a difficult time for the young couple. Dimitry worked hard to provide for his growing family. He and his wife struggled to survive in a foreign country while striving to understand the English language, which Camelia learned by watching television with the aid of a Romanian-English dictionary.

The couple settled in Burbank and awaited the arrival of their firstborn. When the time came, Camelia's labor and delivery went smoothly. So smoothly, in fact, that it left her thinking, "That's it? That's the pain?"

Dominique bounced into the world at a healthy seven pounds six ounces. From the first moment Dimitry saw his little bundle of joy, he thought she looked like a gymnast—which was good, considering the special plans he and Camelia had for their first-born.

"When we got married," Dimitry explained, "we just made a commitment between me and my wife: the first child—whatever it would be—to be a gymnast. If he or she didn't like gymnastics, then, of course, we would have changed sports."

The Moceanus liked the discipline they had learned in gymnastics. Dimitry had been on the Romanian junior national team and Camelia had been a gymnast in grade school. Gymnastics was in their genes, and they hoped that somehow this heritage would be passed along to their children.

To understand the importance of gymnastics in Romania, one must understand the culture and mind-set of its citizens. Gymnastics is the pride of the country. Romanians cannot boast of a world champion soccer team or a world-famous decathlete. However, they do lay claim to a massive pile of Olympic and World Championship medals from gymnastics. For the past two decades this tiny Eastern European nation has been a superpower of the sport. When the country was ruled by the iron fist of a brutal communist regime and the people felt they had nothing, they could still rejoice in the successes of their gymnasts. The athletes brought pride to the hearts of the Romanian people when nothing else could.

The Moceanus decided to test their young daughter's ability in the sport when she was only six months old. Dimitry placed Dominique's tiny hands around a clothesline strung across the kitchen to see if she could hang on. Camelia crouched down on the floor and held her arms out to catch the baby if she fell. Remarkably, tiny Dominique firmly gripped the makeshift bar and did not waver. The line snapped before she would let go. She laughed, thinking it was a fun game.

"She just hung on until the clothesline fell down and we caught her in our arms," Camelia remembered. "We said, 'Wow, she is strong!' "

For Dimitry, the experiment affirmed his daughter's destiny. "See," he said to his wife, "I told you she's going to be a great gymnast."

After he had saved enough money, Dimitry returned to Chicago with his young family and bought Aphrodite's restaurant and a home in the suburbs. When his daughter was three years old, he enrolled her in a recreational gymnastics class in the Chicago area.

"I just got put into a local class and had a lot of fun," Dominique said of her early experiences with the sport. She showed much promise, even from the start. "That was the only thing I ever knew how to do is just flip around."

Her parents wanted her to be a world-class athlete someday and were willing to do whatever it took to attain that goal. "I promised myself . . . [that] I'll make all the sacrifices she needs to be a good gymnast," Dimitry said:

As a young man of sixteen years, Dimitry had been forced to give up gymnastics to concentrate on his studies after much prodding from his parents and teachers. He had long regretted the decision and now wanted to make sure his daughter had the opportunity he had lost. In a way, he saw his daughter's future success in gymnastics as the potential realization of his unfulfilled dream.

But Dominique's gymnastics school was not the kind of place where champions were made, and Dimitry knew it. He had long dreamed of having her coached by the legendary Bela Karolyi, who had opened a gym in Houston, Texas. One day, Dimitry called Bela to ask if he would coach three-and-a-half-year-old Dominique. Bela, who was enormously popular at the time since Mary Lou Retton had just won the 1984 Olympics, had been inundated with requests from parents who wanted him to turn their children into stars.

Bela laughed initially at the request, but when he realized Dimitry was serious, he said, "Let her grow up a little first. Don't make any major family sacrifice."[1]

He suggested the Moceanus wait until Dominique was ten. Normally, he did not coach gymnasts until they were older and more advanced. He let other coaches teach the skills, then he

6

refined them. Bela's strength was not in developing technical ability from scratch. His areas of expertise were perfecting and polishing skills and motivating athletes.

The Moceanus thought Bela was the best. They knew he had shaped Nadia Comaneci and Mary Lou Retton into superstars and believed he could do the same with Dominique. They just needed to find someone to teach her the basics until she was old enough to be trained by Bela.

In the meantime, they did their best to shape Dominique's behavior outside the gym. "My wife stayed home and we watched every step," Dimitry said. "We taught her how to act, how to talk, to have manners. She has very strong manners."[2]

The Moceanus were also careful to preserve their Romanian heritage. They taught Dominique the Romanian language and spoke it at home. Also, Camelia frequently prepared dishes from her native land for dinner.

"I like Romanian foods," Dominique said. "My mom's a good cook and makes food all the time."[3]

After tiring of blisteringly-cold Chicago winters and long hours at the restaurant, the family moved from Illinois to Temple Terrace, Florida, in 1988. Dimitry bought a used-car lot and began managing it.

One of the Moceanus' top priorities upon arriving in Florida was to find a good gym for Dominique. They chose a gymnastics school in nearby Tampa called LaFleur's. The head coach and owner was Jeff LaFleur, a former national gymnast whose family had been heavily involved in the sport. Most of his siblings had been gymnasts, some of whom also owned gymnastics schools in Florida.

Jeff recalled his first encounter with Dimitry and Camelia: "They started the conversation saying they were from Romania and the father was a member of the junior national team, and they would like Dominique to go and train with Bela Karolyi, but he said that she's too young to go there, so they would like me to train her for a while until she gets better."

Jeff accepted Dominique into his program knowing she would leave for Bela's gym one day. Still a beginner, she was initially placed in a regular class, but a month later she was asked to join the pre-team squad. She was not old enough to compete, but she began preparing for competition, which started at age eight. She practiced twice a week for two-and-a-half hours at a time.

Dominique made some lasting first impressions. "When she walked in, you could tell she was going to be good because she was so small and muscular already," observed Becky Waters, one of Dominique's future teammates. "She told us right away she was going to go to Karolyi's as soon as she could and be in the Olympics."

"She was very tiny with a big smile on her face," beam coach Beth Hair remembered, "with big, wide eyes [that said] 'Let me get in here and get going.' She was very energetic, always on the go, always seeking information, and she liked a lot of attention."

Jeff's sister, Toni Rand, who was part owner of the gym at the time, also took notice of little Dominique. "She always smiled, she always seemed to get in a little bit of trouble in workout, and she was a very hard worker and extremely talented."

Like any young gymnast, Dominique sometimes found herself being reprimanded during practice for the usual offenses. "She was a little bit undisciplined at times," Toni laughed, "where she liked to talk a lot—when it was her turn or to the other kids—or maybe wasn't always listening when the coach was talking."

Dominique progressed rapidly, and in the summer of 1989

she was asked to join the team program, starting at level 5. In the U.S. competitive program there are ten levels, with level 1 the lowest and level 10 the highest. Beyond level 10 is a special group called elite, the ultimate ranking possible. Many gymnasts do not aspire to be an elite; a level 9 or 10 gymnast may earn a college scholarship. Only if an athlete's goal is to be on the national team or compete internationally does she seek the highest ranking.

Level 5 gymnasts only do "compulsories"—prescribed routines that must be performed by each athlete on every event to demonstrate technical competence. In a compulsory floor routine, for example, every gymnast performs the same tumbling passes and dance movements to the same music. Watching compulsory competitions can be monotonous, especially when listening to the same music over and over, so they are rarely televised.

Jeff saw a lot of talent in some of his up-and-comers, so he handpicked a few girls—including Dominique—to coach exclusively. He felt so strongly about the potential of this group that he stepped down as coach of the more advanced levels and focused solely on them. Naturally, Dominique's inclusion in the select group meant more hours in the gym. She began practicing five days a week for two-and-a-half hours at a time.

Dominique also experienced another major change in her life. On August 24, 1989, Camelia gave birth to a second child, Christina. Although Dominique was almost eight years older than her sister, she enjoyed playing with her and helping Camelia feed the baby and change diapers.

Shortly after Christina's birth and three weeks after learning the level 5 routines, Dominique competed in her first meet on September 16. Her performance was mediocre and included several falls, largely because she was very tense. She scored a

6.75 on vault, a 7.45 on floor, a 7.75 on bars, and an 8.00 on beam, where she received her first ribbon for eighth place.

"I remember her being pretty nervous," Jeff remarked.

Meets were a lot different from practice for Dominique because she had to contend with judges, fans, and the excitement of competition. She battled nerves in several early contests.

"She actually got so nervous she wet her leotard," Beth recalled about one particular meet.

"I ended up washing them out, rinsing them, and air drying them as best as I possibly could," Jeff's wife Julie LaFleur added. "She got herself back into this very damp leotard because we didn't have any dryers." Despite the incident, Dominique pulled herself together and went on to have a solid performance.

Although she practiced hard, her unfamiliarity with competition caused her to mess up on skills she normally performed well during workout. She had many falls in her first season, but she was gaining valuable experience. She had to get used to competing in different gyms and on different equipment. She also had to adjust to wearing hand grips on bars, which was not easy.

By the end of the season, Dominique became more comfortable in competitions and was able to transfer her performance in practice to the meet. She still struggled with nervousness, but she began to enjoy competing. She also found she liked being the center of attention. Her tomboyish looks—short dark hair, compact frame, sinewy muscles—disguised a charm that came to life only in the gym. Her soft brown eyes blazed when she stepped on the floor. Even as a youngster she made the crowds pay attention when she performed.

"[She was this] little, smiley thing bouncing around from event to event," Toni recalled. "I'm sure for a while she drove the older girls nuts."

"She was young, but pretty tough for a little gal," Jeff

observed. "She qualified to the state meet and by the end of the season was scoring in the 35 range. For an eight year old, that was pretty good."

She won bars and placed second on beam at the Brown's Invitational in October, and she placed fourth overall at the La-Fleur's Invitational in November. The biggest match of her first season was the December state meet. Dominique performed outstandingly well, placing fourth on bars and sixth overall. In the three months since her first meet, her all-around score had jumped more than five points—from a 29.95 to a 35.30.

During competitions, Dominique's mom was often nervous for her daughter. But Dominique's father remained calmly confident in her ability.

"Dimitry was very optimistic and he always believed that she would do good in gymnastics," Camelia said.

This opinion was shared by the coaches at LaFleur's, who noted Dominique's talent early in her career. "She stuck out right away," Toni said. "We knew. There was no doubt. Within six to seven months of her being in the gym, my brother already had an idea that she could make it to the Olympics."

"She had the right body type and had the right genetics working for her," Jeff noted. "Right away you could see some potential there. Probably within about a year we could really see the explosion of talent that was coming out of her."

After the state meet, Dominique moved up to level 6. She began an optional development training program, meaning she tried optional skills for 75% of the time and worked on the level 6 compulsories for the other 25%.

"We recognized then that she was really ready to go," Jeff said. "Of course, the parents were real anxious for her to move as quickly as possible. They were very well schooled in European training systems which were geared toward trying to get the skills acquired in the early ages between seven and eleven. Then we'd start to go into the international scene between twelve and sixteen. At that time I was very much in favor of that idea because the younger kids have more energy, they love the sport, and they love all the flipping and twisting. As they get to be teenagers, it becomes more difficult to do large numbers of skills, so it becomes harder to teach them new skills."

Dominique possessed three key assets that helped her improve rapidly: she enjoyed being in the gym for hours every day, she could do countless repetitions without complaining, and she had no fear. She was able to learn difficult skills easily because of her daredevil attitude that sometimes made the coaches nervous. She lacked that little bit of healthy fear that prevented most kids from trying difficult skills until they were absolutely ready.

"She did not seem to display a whole lot of fear anywhere," Toni remembered. "She was fairly confident in anything that she did, even to the point that you had to be careful what you asked her to do, because even if she wasn't quite ready she might try to do it just because she really wasn't afraid."

"She was great," Jeff commented. "She'd just go to the floor, and I'd say, 'You want a spot?' She'd reply, 'Nah, I've got it.'"

At the age of eight, Dominique could do a whip back to a double twist on floor and a pike Tsukahara on vault. She had giants on bars and a back layout on beam. While the skills came easily to her, she had trouble with her form and needed to learn how to keep her legs straight and her toes pointed at all times. As with most younger gymnasts, she also needed to learn how to dance gracefully on floor.

"She had trouble with self expression on the floor," Jeff explained. "She was more of a mechanical type of gymnast. I think a lot of that was her age. She had trouble bringing out the creativity. I know my wife worked really hard to try to bring out more emotion and personality."

"Her dance was very immature," Julie elaborated. "I wanted the kids to be able to feel their music and put themselves into a character. . . . Her movement was pretty timid."

Dominique also needed to improve her flexibility. Beth worked long and hard on her stretching.

"In the early stage, if she had a weakness, it was with her flexibility," Beth admitted. "We had to work hard on that."

Beth tried to get Dominique's splits down all the way to the ground. Dominique favored splits where her left leg was in front. Like many great gymnasts, including Nadia Comaneci and Shannon Miller, she was right-handed yet left-sided in gymnastics, performing splits and twists to the left and placing her left hand down first on her cartwheel and roundoff.

Dominique's strengths were the acrobatic moves on balance beam and the tumbling on floor, her favorite events. She was also great at uneven bar dismounts. She and Jeff even experimented with a triple back flyaway.

"I'd give her a tap and she'd land on a mat in the pit," Jeff said. "It was pretty cool. It was interesting to see how much she could do at such a young age."

In addition to her tremendous athletic ability, Dominique possessed an easygoing, good-natured demeanor that helped her win favor among people. "When she was eight years old, we went out to a mall to do a tumbling exhibition with the team," Jeff recalled. "She asked me if I would walk her to the ladies' room, so I said, 'Sure, let's go.' As we were approaching the ladies' room there were two elderly ladies approaching the door. Dominique ran around them to apparently get ahead of them. My first reaction was, 'Oh, okay, she's in a hurry.' The reason she ran around them was because she wanted to open the door and hold it for them. And that sort of epitomized Dominique. That's just the way she was."

Her charming personality endeared her to her coaches. "She was wonderful to work with," Beth said. "She'd sit and massage your shoulders or ask how your day was."

Jeff agreed. "She was such a pleasure to be around because she's such a sweet child," he said. "Every day for three years she came in the gym, found me, and gave me a hug. Every day after gym she came over and gave me a hug. Everything was always 'please' and 'thank you' and 'I really appreciate you being my coach.' It was a real pleasure to work with someone with that type of attitude. She was always a very, very hard worker."

Though the coaches loved Dominique, some of her teammates did not share their fondness for the pint-sized daredevil. "I think it was a little bit difficult [for the other kids] to accept how fast Dominique was rising to the top," Jeff acknowledged. "It created a situation that was unusual because she was so good so fast. It became like, 'Wow, how did she do that?'"

Some of the other kids' parents noticed how much Dominique was improving and suspected she was being favored by the coaches. It did not take long for them to bring the issue up with Jeff.

"There was one parent who actually watched practice and counted the number of rotations that Dominique got and everybody else got," claimed Jean Pallardy, a mother of one gymnast. "[Dominique's turns] were a lot more. My daughter didn't want to do that many, so that was fine with me. There were some people that went in and complained about it."

"She took three or four turns before a couple of them had been up once or twice," Beth said. "They just worked a lot slower than she did. She liked to work very quickly. She would say, 'Great, you're not ready. I'll go.'"

"Her work ethic was excellent," Jeff explained. "She had a tremendous capacity for work. She could get off the bar and get right back up with almost little to no rest. She could do more than most any other gymnast I'd seen."

Jeff tried to ease tensions among the parents and avoid disrupting workouts, but to no avail. The disgruntled parents voiced their opinions to their daughters, who began to grow envious of the new rising star.

"There were a lot of jealousies because she learned things very quickly," Beth acknowledged.

When it was time to try a new skill, the coaches often went to Dominique first. Other times, she would be the only one able to master a new move.

"I happened to see a kid compete a Shushunova out of a front handspring and I asked the other kids to do it," Julie recalled. "There was no way they could do it. Well, I asked Dominique to do it, and she could do it the first time. Those kinds of things don't go over well with the other kids."

Jeff tried to quell the rising dissension among his gymnasts. "I tried to keep it to a minimum," he said. He told the girls, "Let's just all work to get as good as we can."

Despite his efforts at diplomacy, Dominique's peers began to treat her differently. She noticed how they whispered behind her back and made snide comments under their breaths. They would mutter things like "Why do you have to go so fast?" or "Slow down!" or "Why do you always have to be first?" Since they did not want to work as fast as Dominique, they began to resent when she led, because then they had to keep pace with her.

Dominique tried not to think about the tension in the gym. "She took everything pretty much in stride," Beth said. "We helped her, telling her, 'It's okay, we all learn at different paces.' She was okay with it. I think she got upset sometimes when the

15

kids would raz her a little bit."

The friction was troubling at points, but Dominique knew why she was in the gym and what she needed to accomplish there. Her parents also helped her to stay focused.

"We say, 'Go work better; forget about yesterday,' " Dimitry stated. "The key to success is to work 100% each day and to do it right once rather than ten times wrong."[4]

"They were very determined for Dominique to be an international gymnast," Jeff said. "They had knowledge about what it took as far as dedication, so they were very determined to get her to practice and be on time, encourage her to work hard, and achieve goals. Their attitude was, 'This is what you're going to do. This is what we're going to do. We're going to make sure you get there, we're going to make sure you work hard, and we're going to make sure you get all the opportunities to succeed.' It made my job easier, actually, to move ahead with her, because she was so dedicated."

Dominique's optimistic personality was similar to that of her mother, who was sweet and soft-spoken. Her father, on the other hand, was more stern and strict. He had a plan for Dominique's life that had begun at her birth, and he was very serious about her gymnastics career.

Some at LaFleur's criticized how Dimitry treated Dominique. They thought he pushed her too hard and demanded too much of her. They also thought he was too intense at competitions and became overly upset if she did not meet his expectations.

"The people in the gym perceived him as a little bit harsh," Jean Pallardy observed. "However, Dominique seemed happy. I think there's that cultural difference, and how much of it is culture and how much of it is personality, I don't know. I think he makes the decisions."

"The dad was pretty outspoken," remarked Jan Spychala, the

mother of another gymnast. "He wanted everyone to know that she was going to be a gymnast and this had been what they had planned for a long time for her. . . . When he came across that strongly, people saw him as being very harsh, because people in America just don't talk about their kids like that. We want them to have a life. We want them to have fun."

"At first I [thought he pushed her too much] because he had her doing conditioning at home," Beth said. "I was always brought up with 'They're kids; let them be children at home.' But it didn't seem to affect her at all."

Dimitry had Dominique do conditioning either in the morning before school or in the evening after practice. Her regimen included situps, pushups, V-ups, handstand pushups, body tighteners, presses to handstand, running up and down the stairs in her townhome, and stretching to improve her flexibility. She also had a bar on which Dimitry had her do pullups and leg lifts.

One of her teammates, Shelly Cavaliere, once spent the night and had to do some conditioning with Dominique. "He times you and you have to do a lot," she remembered. "I'd be scared not to do a lot because he would yell or something."

While Dominique's father instructed her at home, her parents let Jeff do the coaching in the gym. "They didn't try to tell me how to coach at all," he emphasized. "I've got to hand it to them, because they probably knew enough that they could have tried to, but they didn't. The only thing they did ask for was more [workout] time."

"Dominique's parents had a certain goal for her," Beth said, "and I think it was Dominique's goal, too. She was working with her parents and coaches to achieve her goal. I think her goals were a little higher than some of the other children."

Dominique's aspirations and those of her parents were intertwined. In fact, they would often set her goals for her. She had been begging her parents to let her grow her hair long, but they told her she had to make the national team first.

Every once in a while the pressure got to her. "She would come into the gym crying sometimes," Reneé Barnett, a teammate, confessed. "Her dad wanted her to do more and more. Her dad wanted her to move up to elite and she wasn't there yet. I think that's when he kept pushing and pushing her."

But Dominique was a people pleaser. She tried her hardest to keep everyone happy—parents, coaches, teammates. These people were her support group.

While she respected her parents' high expectations, her own ambition was her primary motivation. She wanted to be in the gym and she wanted to be the best.

Chapter 2

Leaving

I n the fall of 1990, Dominique began competing at level 6. She had an impressive start, winning the vault at her first two local meets. She also had strong finishes at the Gemini and LaFleur's Invitationals. To cap off the stellar season, in December she was crowned Florida State Champion on uneven bars.

After the state meet, she skipped level 7 and went into level 8 where she would be required for the first time to perform optional routines, or "optionals," instead of compulsories. In optionals, each gymnast performs unique routines created exclusively for her that showcase her abilities. These meets are more interesting to watch since everyone has different routines and music.

The level 8 season started in January, leaving Dominique

only a month to switch gears from compulsories and get ready for optionals. In her first optional meet she was a little jittery and placed sixth. But by the time her second meet rolled around a few weeks later, she was ready. She achieved the highest score on bars and the second highest on vault. She had a fall on beam but still managed to win the all-around with a 35.70. Dominique could not have been more pleased with her first all-around victory. She kept the momentum going with a win at sectionals, the qualifying competition for the state meet.

Although her rapid rise to the top was met with petty jealousies along the way, Dominique became good friends with two of her level 8 teammates, Shelly Cavaliere and Becky Wildgen. The three chums hung out together even though both Shelly and Becky were several years Dominique's senior.

Sometimes they fooled around at the coaches' expense. "We had this coach together one time," Shelly remembered. "All of us hated him. Dominique would teach us words in Romanian—bad words, I guess—and we would say funny things to him. He would have no clue what we were talking about."

Dominique enjoyed competing with her friends. Within three months, she became one of the best level 8 gymnasts in Florida and qualified to the 1991 state meet in March. She had problems on bars, scoring a dismal 8.00, but she roared back with a 9.40 on beam—the top score of the day—and a 9.25 on floor. She placed fifth in the all-around and advanced to regionals, the highest meet to which a level 8 could qualify. Teammate Tara Tagliarino won the children's division, and Dominique's club placed second overall.

The regional meet, held a month later in Nashville, was a competition between the top athletes from Florida and the seven nearby states of Alabama, Georgia, Louisiana, Mississippi, North Carolina, South Carolina, and Tennessee. Dominique scored

35.65 total points, placing second in the individual all-around by a tenth to Susie Krug of the American Twisters. Dominique's uneven bar routine, which included a sky-high double back flyaway dismount, was good enough for a 9.05 and first place on the event. She placed second on vault, third on beam, and fourth on floor.

Flush with success as a level 8, Dominique decided with her coaches it was time to try for elite. She joined Jeff's elite squad, which consisted of four other members: Reneé Barnett, Leila Pallardy, Emily Spychala, and Becky Waters. This group's summer workouts were increased to twice a day.

Dominique took practice seriously. "Her father *never* let her miss gym," Beth stated. "She was *always* here unless she was very ill."

While Jeff wanted his gymnasts to enjoy the sport, he expected and demanded a lot from them. Sometimes he got angry and yelled, "You need to try harder!" If he felt they were fooling around too much, he or Beth would ask them to leave. Everyone got kicked out once in a while.

"He was definitely rough," Emily said of Jeff's coaching style, "but Dominique seemed to handle him okay. The rest of us got more upset than she did. He pushed real hard . . . and yelled at all of us."

The extra practice took some getting used to, but it really improved Dominique's skill level. On vault she learned a front handspring front pike somersault and a handspring front with a half twist. She also started working on a full-twisting tucked Yurchenko. On floor she mastered a full-twisting double back somersault and a triple twist, and on beam she practiced two consecutive layouts, a roundoff back handspring layout, and a roundoff double back dismount. She learned a Gienger and a full-twisting giant swing on bars, and Jeff taught her how to swing quickly around the high bar before her dismount.

"I spent a lot of time getting her to tap her giant over the top of the bar," he said, "and she loved it. The faster I would whip her around the bar, the more she liked it."

Despite age differences, Dominique became very close with her teammates. For her tenth birthday she invited them all over to her place one Saturday after practice. Her parents rented a party room at the clubhouse by the pool. Everyone played games, swam, and ate birthday cake. There were lots of presents. Dominique had a great time.

Her birthday celebration was a special occasion. Normally, her parents sheltered her from a lot of distracting social functions outside the gym.

"They kept her away from the mainstream of a lot of parties or social stuff," Jean Pallardy remarked. "They said, '*This* is your focus,' and she prospered."

Because of this isolation, Dominique did not experience some of the things other kids did. "The first time we went on an out-of-state trip, she didn't know what so many things were," Becky Waters recalled. "She didn't know what salad dressing was, bacon bits, sour cream, or any of that fattening stuff. We went to a restaurant and the waiter asked what she wanted on her baked potato. We were all like, 'Just say plain.' I'm not sure how bad it is [not to have fattening food] because none of us were allowed to eat it anyway. I kind of wish I hadn't known what it was, because then I wouldn't have missed it."

Dominique's mom usually prepared Romanian food for the family, but once in a while she took Dominique to fast food restaurants. Her parents were careful to monitor the fats and sweets their daughter ate, offering her delicious homemade bread in place of the junk food eaten as snacks by most kids. Still,

Dominique developed quite a sweet tooth.

"Her parents didn't let her eat a lot of foods like potato chips and stuff like that," Reneé said. "She loved candy. Any time she could get her hands on some candy, she did."

Dominique liked going over to other kids' houses because they had foods her mom usually did not make. She was particularly fond of chocolate. Brownies and Reese's Peanut Butter Cups were among her favorites.

"I remember one time when I had her and Shelly Cavaliere spend the night," Becky Wildgen said. "My mom had just made a whole bunch of cupcakes. Shelly and I went down to go get some and they were all gone. We were like, 'Where did they go?' And Dominique said, 'Oops, I ate them.' She had like twelve of them."

"She said she never had any before," Shelly laughed.

The friendships Dominique enjoyed with her teammates and coaches helped her improve as a gymnast and grow as a person. Their support also helped her and her family through a tough situation. Once, when the Moceanus were away on vacation, Dimitry suffered a serious business loss.

"He left his car dealership in the hands of a friend," Julie remembered. "Well, the friend sold everything, took the money, and left them with nothing—at least that's the story that Dimitry gave us."

This "friend" put the Moceanus in severe financial trouble. Fortunately, Jeff was understanding and told them they could pay whatever they could afford for Dominique's lessons. They also had difficulty handling the travel expenses for away meets, and Jeff offered to pick up the tab when they could not.

"When we would get to the hotel, she would get this sad face sometimes," Reneé admitted. "I would be like, 'What's wrong?' 'Well, my dad didn't send me any money.' Sometimes I would give her some money because I felt bad."

While Dimitry drove various nice cars from his dealership, he maintained a modest lifestyle, scraping together what he could to pay for his daughter's gymnastics.

Dominique began her third competitive season with the goal of becoming an elite gymnast and making the U.S. junior national team. She practiced four-and-a-half hours after school and on Saturdays. Since she was skipping two levels, Jeff had to write a petition describing her skills so she would be allowed to compete in the elite trial meet.

To become an elite, Dominique had to receive a minimum score of 34.50 at an elite national element testing. From there she would advance to the elite regionals, normally called "zones." She needed to score at least a 36.00 to qualify for either the U.S. or American Classic, and depending on her placement at one of these meets she could make it to the U.S. Championships, the top national meet of the year.

In her first try for elite, Dominique faltered, suffering two falls on beam and one on bars. As a result, she came up a few tenths short of qualifying to zones. She and her family were very disappointed, but Jeff was not ready to give up. He approached the judges and explained Dominique's predicament. They re-evaluated her scores on each event and bumped up her all-around total by a couple tenths, allowing her to narrowly qualify to the regional meet.

Dominique was thankful for the opportunity to compete at zones on October 20 at Brown's Gymnastics. She had a much better competition, scoring a 9.20 on vault, a 9.15 on bars, an 8.75 on beam, and a 9.10 on floor. Her solid effort earned her a spot at Classics.

She traveled to Salt Lake City, Utah, in early November for

her first major elite competition as a junior, the 1991 American Classic. She had some problems, including falls on beam and floor, and she finished seventh overall with 36.425 points.

Her teammate, Leila, won the meet. Leila was a couple years older than Dominique, but the two were friends. Leila thought of Dominique as her little sister.

Leila's mother recalled an amusing incident that occurred during the girls' stay in Utah: "Leila told Dominique, 'Whatever you do, don't sit on the toilet seat in the airplane and in the rest rooms in the airport.' I'm a nurse and I stress hygiene. So they're in the hotel room and they notice that it's kind of messy in the bathroom. My daughter said, 'What the heck? Somebody is not hitting the toilet here.' And Dominique said, 'Well, you told me not to ever sit down.' "

Dominique was the youngest elite gymnast from the state of Florida and one of the youngest elites ever in the United States. In two years she had gone from an entry-level gymnast in level 5 to the top echelon of the sport.

Dimitry could see how much Dominique had improved and realized his daughter needed the best possible coaching to reach her full potential. He believed Bela Karolyi was the finest coach in the world and wondered if now was the time to move Dominique to Houston. Coincidentally, Dominique began to wonder the same thing.

One afternoon, she sat mesmerized in front of the television watching a gymnastics meet, the 1991 World Championships. She was impressed by Bela's enthusiasm and big bear hugs. She noticed that he coached most of the gymnasts on the U.S. team and saw how solid and physically prepared they were. One in particular was in a class by herself. She enthralled the crowd, especially on floor, with her spectacular tumbling and winning smile. She made the most difficult maneuvers seem effortless. She was America's first World All-Around Champion, Kim Zmeskal.

Dominique longed to be as good as Kim, to be the envy of budding young gymnasts everywhere, and she knew where she needed to train to fulfill her ambitions. During the broadcast, she turned to her father and told him that she wished she could train at Karolyi's.

Dimitry did not hesitate: "Okay, let's go."

Dominique could not believe her ears.

A short time later, over Thanksgiving weekend, the family took a trip. Dimitry did not tell Dominique where they were going.

"We just told her we were going on a vacation for a few days, and a couple of days later we arrived at Bela Karolyi's," he said. "She was like, 'What a surprise!' "

Bela had to evaluate Dominique and put her through a series of tests to see if she could handle his strenuous program. "The most important is the obstacle course," he observed. "All the girls start together, and they must climb a rope, run across the beam, tumble—things like this. It tests agility, speed, and will-power. The one I want is the one who is pulling back the other ones, clawing with her fingers, and biting to get in front. She's a fighter."[1]

With his imposing height, fierce countenance, and sharp tongue, Bela was quite an intimidating character to a young girl. Dominique resolved to try her hardest to impress this coach whom she knew to be a maker of champions.

It worked. Her spunk caught his eye, and she was accepted into his program. Needless to say, the Moceanus were elated. They had been waiting almost a decade for this moment.

Without hesitation, they decided to uproot the family and

make the move to Houston. "We knew this would be expensive," Dimitry admitted. "But we said, 'Even if we don't have money to eat, even if we have to drink water and eat bread and salt, we're going to do it.' "[2]

Tuition at Karolyi's was over $300 a month. Travel expenses, meet entry fees, leotards, grips, shoes, and private lessons were all additional. It was very expensive, but the Moceanus were willing to make the sacrifices. They believed that if Dominique made the national team, she would be able to obtain sponsors to help pay for training.

After returning to Tampa, Dominique could not tell Jeff where she had been. He did not like his elite students training at other gymnastics schools.

There was much to be done in preparation for the move. The Moceanus had to pack their belongings. Camelia had to quit her job at a beauty salon. Dimitry decided to stay behind for the time being because he was reluctant to sell his used-car dealership. He planned to join the family in Houston as soon as he could. Camelia and Dominique hoped they would not have to be separated from him for long. Dominique enjoyed a special relationship with her father and wanted the family to be together as soon as possible.

Dominique competed in her last meet with LaFleur's in December. She and her teammates traveled south to Miami for the Junior Orange Bowl Invitational where she finished tenth overall. She qualified to two event finals and finished third on beam with a 9.10 and seventh on vault with a 9.30.

Throughout Dominique's time at LaFleur's, Dimitry had openly admitted that he thought Bela was the best. He had often declared his intentions to have Dominique train with Bela. As a result, people had always expected the Moceanus to leave eventually, but the suddenness of their departure came as a surprise.

"We were at workout, and she said she had this big secret," Emily remembered. "She made us guess. I was like, 'You're moving to another gym,' just playing around. And then she said, 'Yeah, I'm going to Karolyi's.' I was like, 'Oh, my gosh.' It was a big shock, because we were real close. It was scary, because we were like one big family."

Although some of Dominique's teammates knew about her upcoming move, she still had not told Jeff. At an exhibition on Friday, December 20, she entered the gym knowing this was her last day.

"She was not even going to tell Jeff, but we made her go tell him," Becky Wildgen claimed. "She just went up and told him in between events."

Jeff did not take the news well. "When he found out, he was all upset and called her in for a meeting," Emily said. "She was just going to leave like it was no big deal. He was like, 'You're leaving?!' He thought it was a big joke, I guess."

According to some of her friends, Dominique had not been told it was her last day until that very morning because her parents thought Jeff would try to persuade her to stay.

"He had a way of talking people out of things," Becky Wildgen observed.

Dominique could not bear to see Jeff so upset. It was tearing her apart. She did not want to leave her friends and coaches, but she knew Bela was the coach best able to advance her career. As long as she could remember, her father had been telling her how great Bela was.

"Her dad was the main reason she wanted to go," Becky Waters suggested.

"She said she didn't want to go, but I think she did want to go inside," Shelly said. "She hated to leave all of her friends, but then again she knew she could get better at gymnastics."

As Dominique stood by the door for the last time, her team-mates encircled her in a farewell embrace and wished her well. There wasn't a dry eye in the bunch.

"We were never going to see her again," Emily said quietly, "so it was sad."

It was a difficult moment for Dominique. She was going to miss her teammates and coaches very much. Beth gave her a picture of herself that Dominique would keep in her room for many years. She promised to keep in touch with everyone.

When her parents arrived to pick her up, Jeff asked to speak with them. After all he had done for them, he could hardly believe they were just going to leave without giving any notice or saying goodbye. The group somberly stepped into his office to discuss the matter.

"I had a meeting with the parents and Dominique," Jeff recalled, "and they said, 'Well, she's going to go work at Bela's.' And I said, 'Okay.' It was real emotional; we were just so close. I think for all of us, we loved Dominique. I think she legitimately was very, very close with us. There was a strong emotional attachment. We spent every day with her for almost three years. It was difficult. There were a lot of tears in that meeting."

"He put a lot of emotion into [coaching] her," Jean Pallardy revealed. "I think he was hoping that maybe he could prove that he could do it and they wouldn't want to move."

"He saw how special she was," noted Jan Spychala, Emily's mother. "He really thought he could be the one to bring her as far as she wanted to go. I think he felt bad that they felt he couldn't do it and she had to go somewhere else to achieve it."

The coaches had assumed Dominique would probably stay at least through 1992. They had received no indication she was leaving until the last day. While they had believed she would go to Karolyi's *someday*, her sudden departure left them shocked and deeply hurt.

"It was a sore spot with us," Julie admitted, "because we knew that she didn't want to go. In fact, they didn't even *really* tell us—they just left."

"We thought she went a little early," Beth said. "I wish she would have waited just a little longer."

The next day at practice, those in the group who had not been at the exhibition found out about Dominique's departure. Jeff huddled everyone together and told them. Some cried; they were upset that they had not been given a chance to say goodbye.

"None of us could believe she had just left like that," Becky Wildgen said. "It was such a surprise. We all knew she was going to leave someday. We all had that feeling, but we weren't expecting it yet."

Becky Waters added, "Working out that long with someone in a small group, you have a special bond you can't really explain. You're pulling for that other person when they're injured, and you know how hard everyone is trying. For someone just to leave is like part of you is gone, too, because you cared so much about that person and then they're just gone."

Jeff spent the entire Saturday morning practice session lecturing and talking through the ordeal with his students. He, his coaching staff, and the team needed to sort out their feelings.

"We all wanted to talk about why she left," Reneé said, "and why her parents made her leave, because everybody liked her."

Jeff spoke for hours. He asked the girls if they should let Dominique come back if she chose to return. He also told them not to go to Karolyi's, because Bela was too strict and mean. Everyone had suspected Dominique would eventually move there, but they had not anticipated Jeff's reaction.

"He was talking about that we should never leave," Emily recalled. "He was really upset about it. He didn't like Karolyi's at all. He thought his coaching was wrong. He forbade us to go there. Leila and I [admitted we had gone] to camp there, and he went ballistic. He was extremely upset. The whole gym was crying."

Over the next several weeks, Jeff seemed more agitated than usual with his athletes, and his mood and tone became much more negative. Finally, several parents had had enough. Leila and Emily's mothers went in to speak with him.

"Jeff just seemed out of sorts," Jean remembered. "I thought, 'What's the problem? Is he pining away after Dominique?' I went in and talked to Jeff and said, 'Listen. Dominique's there. Face it. But you have kids out there depending on you, so get with the program.' He goes, 'No, no, that's not it.' And I said, 'Oh, baloney.' He said, 'Well, yeah, it's going to be hard seeing her at the Classic with another gym.' "

"He was a mess," Jan agreed. "He was so down. The whole gym was down. It was very depressing."

Eventually, Jeff came to grips with the realization that Dominique was not coming back. While he did not agree with Bela's philosophy, he knew Dominique could achieve her goals under him.

"I knew that Bela was actually going to follow through with Dominique's plan," Jeff said. "If he was going to be the strategist behind her training, then . . . I knew that it was going to be in her best interest."

Within two years, the remaining elite squad at LaFleur's would disperse. Leila and Becky would eventually tire of the constant pressure and turn to track, Emily would switch gyms and then go into diving, and Reneé would quit altogether.

While the LaFleur's gym was undergoing its turmoil, the Moceanus were embarking on a new adventure that would forever change their lives. They packed up and drove west, arriving in Houston shortly before Christmas. Camelia and her two girls found a convenient place to live—a house next door to the gym—from which Dominique could walk to practice. Bela owned the house as well as one on the other side of the gym that he rented to coaches and athletes.

Just outside the cozy, mustard-colored gym located in a quiet suburban area of north Houston, the ambiance was deceptively peaceful. Inside, sparks flew as tiny airborne pixies flipped and twisted furiously across the floor and around the bars and down the beam. Each was hoping to catch Bela's eye and be chosen for his elite squad—the top six or seven girls in the gym and maybe the country.

Dominique was nervous as she stepped inside the famous training center for her first day of practice. Karolyi's consisted of three gyms: a recreational gym, a team gym, and an elite gym. Only Bela's hand-picked elite team was allowed to work out in the latter.

The elite gym was equipped with a vault, a spring floor, three sets of bars, four beams, and a tumble-track packed tightly in one corner. Its light-blue walls were lined with mirrors and perforated by several tiny windows and a garage door which Bela opened during the humid summers. The flags of the United States and the state of Texas were prominently displayed, and hanging on the wall between two banners for a gym sponsor, the Olympic flag served as a constant reminder of the gymnasts' ultimate goal.

The team gym, which would become Dominique's second home, had a row of seven balance beams, a vault, two sets of uneven bars, a single bar, and a spring floor. Posters representing the major television networks—NBC SportsWorld, ABC's Wide World of Sports, and CBS Sports—were strung across the gym's white walls along with sponsor names like Continental Airlines,

Gallery Furniture, McDonald's, and Reebok.

A tiny observation room between the team and elite gyms allowed parents to watch their daughters train and compete. Above this room was a dance studio where the elites took two half-hour dance classes a week.

Before Dominique could begin, she had to be evaluated and placed in the proper group. "On her first day at the gym, we had practice in our own [elite] gym and she was in there," recalled Betty Okino, an elite gymnast and future Olympian. "I can't remember why she was in there, because no one ever came in our gym. I think she was coming to try out. We were on beam and she was in the corner of the floor tumbling, making up little floor routines, doing handstands, and trying to copy what we were doing on beam."

Dominique's outstanding ability was recognized immediately, and she was placed in the junior elite group with several other kids her age who were aiming for the 1996 Olympics in Atlanta, Georgia. The junior elites were the future superstars next in line to be coached by Bela. In this group Dominique met several talented youngsters: Monica Flammer, Tanya Maiers, Jamie Martini, Stephanie Robbins, Amanda Seaholm, Jennie Thompson, and two girls from Guatemala, Rocio Salazar and Javiera Castellon. Since Bela only coached the top handful, Dominique and the other junior elites were coached by James Holmes, who had been asked to take over after Bela fired well-known national coach Rick Newman. James had been with Bela for many years, starting as a janitor and eventually working his way up to elite coach.

James was impressed with Dominique from the beginning. "She was really talented, strong, and aggressive," he observed. "We were real impressed with the power. At that point she just seemed to be a little bit sloppy. She came very young but real high in skill quality."

James remembered trying to teach Dominique a full-twisting double back flyaway off bars: "Certain times she would let go of that release for the dismount—she looked like a cat thrown up in the air—and she could land on her feet somehow. In the middle of it we're thinking, 'Oh my God, Dominique's going to kill herself!' Then she's on her feet and we're going, 'Hey, how did you do that? You scared me, you little guy!' You honestly thought, 'Oh my goodness! How am I going to recover this and grab this kid?' Then she's on her feet looking up at you going, 'Hey, did you see that?' . . . We were always amazed at some of the things she did, and she would go, 'Oh yeah, I just did it.' The dismount was particularly funny, because there were times that she got a little wild and we did have to chase her down a little bit."

Dominique had to learn how to hit her routines every time without falling. "In the very beginning, especially, she sometimes would throw these amazing dismounts and then the next time shoot twenty feet forward," James said. "You're saying, 'Hey buddy, listen. If you continue to do this and someone has to grab you, you're going to knock your head off, and then you can't train.' You try to be persistent and not too abusive as far as intimidating the athlete, but you have to make them understand the fear and respect that a bad one can create a problem, and problems mean you're not able to train."

In addition to upgrading some of her tricks and gaining consistency, Dominique had to learn a floor routine befitting her new team's style. Bela had top choreographer Geza Pozsar flown in to create his elites' floor routines. Once a professional ballet dancer in Romania, Geza owned a gym in Sacramento called Pozsar's Gymnastics. He came to Karolyi's once a month and more frequently as major competitions approached. Geza had begun working with Bela in 1974, and both had defected together in 1981.

When Geza was in town, Dominique had one-hour private lessons with him each day to work on both compulsory and optional floor and beam dance. While working on her new floor routine for the first time, they ran into some difficulties with the dance.

"I was trying to put together a floor routine for her when she first came, and she couldn't get the beat," Geza said. "There was no way I could get her to be with the music. She was off all the time."

"I was supposed to dance in a circle," Dominique explained, "counting off the steps—one, two, three, four, five, six, seven, eight—and then jump into a little pose. *Not* a difficult program. *Anyone* could do this. Anyone except me, as it turned out. No matter how I tried, I couldn't get the eight steps just right, and I couldn't figure out how to do the pose the right way."[3]

Kim and Betty tried to help, but by demonstrating the sequence perfectly on the first run through, they only humiliated Dominique more. Nothing was working.

"Bela got mad," Geza said. "He ran over from the bars and started to jump up and down to show her. He got impatient with her. Both of us were jumping up and down around her just to make her do a few very simple steps. It was Russian music. It was supposed to be very easy, but she didn't get it. She wasn't exactly what you'd call a natural dancer."

Dominique found it difficult to connect the dance segments fluidly. She lacked formal dance training, and it showed. Geza spent many hours turning her feet out, straightening her posture, showing her how to hold her hands correctly, and lifting her head so she would not look at the floor. Eventually, she began to make progress, but it took a lot of private lessons and dance classes with Geza.

While Dominique missed her old coaches, she was becoming more familiar with her new ones.

"She was a neat kid," James said. "She was funny, always happy, and you could joke around with her. She would laugh, play around, and enjoy the workout. She was real aggressive and competitive against the other kids. Like most real talented kids, she was hardheaded and didn't like to be told things weren't done correctly in the beginning. I think she came from a gym where she was the star. She walked into Karolyi's where she was just another *hopeful* star."

Dominique quickly realized who was the best of the squad: Jennie Thompson. She and Jennie became friends, but they also competed against each other in the gym daily. The healthy competition spurred them on and improved their gymnastics. When Jennie was catching her release moves on bars, Dominique wanted to catch all of hers. Likewise, when Dominique was nailing all of her beam sets, Jennie wanted to do the same. Bela's system thrived on friendly rivalries.

"All of the great gymnasts in the past have always had one," Betty explained. "Mary Lou Retton and Dianne Durham, Kristie Phillips and Phoebe Mills, me and Kim Zmeskal, and then Jennie and Dominique."

The pair did things outside the gym as well. Sometimes they spent the night at each other's houses. They liked to watch movies, go to the mall, rollerblade, or just hang out together.

"We lived in the same neighborhood," Jennie said. "We would ride bikes together and stuff."

While they had similar interests, their personalities were vastly different. Jennie was quiet, shy, and serious. A meticulous worker, she was in the gym to get her job done as efficiently as possible. Her intensity inspired the others to keep up. Dominique, on the other hand, was bubbly and outgoing. She lightened the mood and made practice fun. Still, her raw talent kept her neck-and-neck with Jennie. Dominique was quick and powerful, while Jennie was flexible and coordinated.

"Both Jennie and Dominique were the kind of kids—you had two people willing to make the same sacrifices with different personalities—that would jump back up [on the beam after splitting it]," James remarked. "When you get kids side by side doing that, you create monsters. What kind of push is that? If they fall on their layout, they're back up trying five more, then they go over there and say, 'Oh man, look what I did to my leg.'

"Bela had the power and the presence to get these people together. These are kids that have goals set and aspirations that some adults don't have, at eight, nine, ten, and eleven years old. When I was ten years old, I was on my bicycle barefoot all day long. These kids are really working, striving, and sacrificing for that. Two kids like that together—you can't help but be successful. And I think the kids knew that."

In spite of their young age, the two rivals were intensely focused. "If you want to get anything you have to work hard at it," Jennie declared. "Just set your goals and work for them. I just try to do my best. I probably push myself the hardest."

Dominique and Jennie each aspired to become the best in the group. Only time would tell which one came out on top.

Chapter 3

Bela

Dominique's first competition as a member of the Karolyi clan was the Alamo City Invitational held February 23, 1992 in San Antonio, Texas. Competing against the veterans of her team, Dominique placed ninth overall. Reigning World Champion Kim Zmeskal, who was five-and-a-half years Dominique's senior, captured the all-around title as expected.

"All the little guys stood out above even Kim Zmeskal at that time," coach James Holmes said. "Dominique came in and just nailed a beam routine, and that instantly captivated the audience, who thought, 'Hey, these little guys are chasing the big ones and making it tough on them.' They didn't beat that team, but they definitely stole some of the limelight from that group."

The Karolyi A team, Bela's top guns, demolished the rest of

the field in the team competition. Although Dominique was on the B team, which placed third, it was exciting to be a member of such a prestigious group.

"We really didn't place very high, but we had fun," fellow teammate Monica Flammer recalled. "We thought we were cool to compete with them, because they were the best ones."

In April, Dominique went to the U.S. Classic in Knoxville, Tennessee. She did not do as well as she had hoped, finishing tenth in the all-around and fourth on beam. She did, however, qualify to the U.S. Championships to be held a month later in Columbus, Ohio.

At the Classic she saw the crew from LaFleur's for the first time since she had left. There was an unspoken rivalry between Dominique and her old teammates. The LaFleur's girls had something to prove—that Jeff was an excellent coach and his team could keep pace with Bela's. Leila Pallardy placed higher than Dominique, but Emily Spychala did not.

Ever since the Moceanus' abrupt move to Houston, tension had existed between them and the coaches at LaFleur's. However, the relationship seemed to be mended at the meet. Dominique's parents and former coaches exchanged hugs, and Dominique gave Beth Hair a warm embrace and thanked her for the great job she had done coaching beam.

Dominique disobeyed Bela by speaking with her old coaches. "She was told under no circumstances should she talk to us by Bela," Julie LaFleur claimed.

Jeff and Julie were saddened to learn of Bela's instructions. They missed Dominique a lot and knew she still missed them as well. She had even sent them letters on occasion, writing about the difficulty of adjusting to the move.

"Since I've worked out for a little bit now, I'm used to the yelling and I don't cry anymore," she wrote in one letter a month after leaving. "I still have to work out without the bars wet," she complained, referring to her old gym's practice of spraying the bars with water that was not allowed at Karolyi's. "I'm sort of used to it, but not a lot. I miss you all very much."

Shortly after the U.S. Classic, Dominique and Jennie were asked to join Bela's prestigious circle of elites. They began training alongside their heroes Kim Zmeskal, Betty Okino, Kerri Strug, and Hilary Grivich. Dominique idolized and tried to emulate Kim the most.

Besides the anxiety that came with practicing next to world champions, Dominique experienced the nervousness of performing under Bela's direction and scrutiny. "It's pretty intimidating when you first come to Karolyi's and you've seen him on TV," Kerri explained. "He's such a great coach, and then to actually have him start coaching you is scary at first."

"I was scared he wouldn't like me," Dominique said. She knew about Bela's long history of training top athletes from Nadia Comaneci to Mary Lou Retton to Phoebe Mills to Kim Zmeskal, and she wanted to make a good impression.

"I remember thinking that she had a lot of talent and she could do a lot of skills for being that young," Hilary said, describing her first impressions of Dominique. "She was doing some of the same skills I was, and I had been in gymnastics a long time, so I was pretty impressed with her."

Dominique watched as her older teammates trained for the 1992 Olympics, which were only a few months away. She was eager for her chance in the spotlight, but she had to mature and upgrade her skills.

"Being coached by the greatest is really a dream come true," she said. "I never thought I would make it here to Karolyi's."

At LaFleur's, Dominique had been the center of attention. At

Karolyi's, she was just another talented gymnast. Bela focused more on Kim and Betty than he did on Dominique and Jennie. But that did not stop Dominique from working hard in practice.

Under Bela, Dominique's workout hours increased. She practiced twice a day, Monday through Saturday. In an average morning workout, she did oversplits—one leg on mats and the other on the floor—to stretch her legs more than 180 degrees. She easily worked through several presses to handstand and some light tumbling, then she ran laps around the floor mat for about thirty minutes, sometimes turning to go backwards, then sideways, then lifting her knees as high as possible. Next came conditioning exercises for an hour or more. With weights around her ankles, she did hundreds of situps, pushups, V-ups, and arch-ups.

The first part was just a warmup. The real workout began with six or seven compulsory uneven bar and balance beam routines, two or three compulsory floor routines, and many compulsory vaults. That is, *if* she were hitting them. If not, she had to do more routines until her coaches were satisfied.

In the evening, Dominique returned to complete six or seven optional uneven bar and balance beam routines, and two or three full optional floor routines. The same rule applied as in the morning: if the routines were good, she did not have to do as many. She then practiced her vaults until Bela felt she had done enough. Optionals involved more difficult skills and took more endurance to perform.

Bela could be heard barking "Harder, harder!" during the tumbling exercises. Once in a while, he complimented someone with a "Good," but most of the time he called out "What are you doing?" or "It's no good! Do it right!"

At the end of the evening workout, the girls did a little more conditioning. On the bars they did pullups, chinups, leg lifts, pirouettes, and casts to handstand. They also did reverse leg lifts, hanging upside down on the low bar and lifting their torsos, while Bela watched closely for any cheaters trying to get away with doing less than the number of repetitions he had specified.

Dominique and Jennie were intimidated by Bela at first. "We were scared of him," Jennie admitted. "We did whatever he told us to do." They had a little trouble understanding his thick Romanian accent, but they got used to it after a while.

Bela was very demanding, and Dominique's routines never seemed good enough. There were always corrections to be made, especially with her form. Bela was constantly telling her to keep her legs "tight"—together and straight.

Sometimes she did not understand what Bela wanted. "What am I doing wrong?" she wondered. "I don't know why you're yelling at me."[1]

Bela summarized his coaching philosophy in a few poignant words: "My attitude is never to be satisfied, never enough. The girls must be little tigers—clawing, kicking, biting, roaring to the top. They stop for one minute—poof!—they are finished."[2]

Although Bela was harsh at times, Dominique listened closely to what he had to say. She realized that attention was not given to slackers. If she did not show improvement or try her hardest, she was ignored. If she got a large rip on her hand from the bars and showed it to Bela, he would acknowledge it then say, "Let's try the skill again." Dominique also quickly learned that when Bela said to do "just one more," she was about halfway through her workout.

When she was injured and unable to practice, an alternative workout was arranged. For example, if she had hurt her wrist, Bela would make her run a couple of miles so the rest of her body would still get a workout and she would not lose any endurance. If Bela thought any gymnast was not doing her assigned conditioning, he kicked her out of the gym or made her pull an eight-inch crash mat up and down the vaulting runway as punishment.

It seemed like everyone got kicked out of the gym at one time or another. Jennie was once kicked out as she was walking to the beam to start her workout. Unable to find her roll of tape, she had been the last one out of the locker room. Bela did not like anyone trailing behind because it made them seem unmotivated and unwilling to work hard.

Dominique was occasionally kicked out as well. Bela asked her to leave when he was not satisfied with her performances or when he thought she was not trying hard enough.

"He is so mean to me!" Dominique would sometimes exclaim to Jennie. However, when Bela kicked her out of the gym, she often fought back. "I want to do bars!" she would protest.

Sometimes, Bela would relent: "I'll give you a second chance, then."[3] Jennie, who was not so bold in talking back to the coach, thought this was unfair. But other times Bela insisted that Dominique leave. He did not kick his athletes out of the gym that frequently, because then they missed valuable workout time. Only if he became very angry or the gymnast was endangering herself did he resort to expulsion.

No matter how injured, tired, or sick the gymnasts were, everyone was expected to attend practice. If someone had the flu, she was expected to do what everyone else was doing. No one was pampered. It was highly unusual for someone to miss a scheduled workout.

"That's why his gymnasts were always the strongest," Betty claimed. "We can push ourselves through the worst of days and the best of days. You never know how you are going to feel on the day of the Olympics. You could be sick that day, and that one workout you were throwing up and sick and Bela kept pushing you and making you do everything is going to make all the difference."

Once in a while a gymnast would get fed up with the arduous workouts and switch gyms. Several members of Dominique's junior elite squad had already left to join other clubs.

Practice was serious and intense. Bela demanded perfection. Music and talking were not allowed, so Dominique was quiet and barely said anything. The only voice that could be heard was Bela's: "Now Dominique, ready? Let's do it one more time." When she did her floor routine in practice, Bela could be heard yelling "Watch your back handspring" or "Strong, strong, strong!" or "Punch it!"

"Any workout with Bela is tough and disciplined," Hilary said. "It's a different mentality than it is in the lower groups. Dominique had to adjust to that so it was hard for her at first. It's not that it's not as much fun, but you have to be more disciplined in the workouts. You can't talk and you have to really pay attention at *all* times during the *entire* workout."

Dominique would sometimes get discouraged in practice when she was trying to learn new skills and make the improvements Bela wanted, but it was just not working. At such times, her attitude angered Bela, which only made matters worse. Dominique was already frustrated with herself, and Bela's criticism only compounded the problem.

"Why is he getting mad at me?" she would think to herself. "I know I can't do it. I'm working on it."

"If he was stern with her or if he was trying to get her to make a certain correction and she would get frustrated and upset, he didn't like for that to happen," Hilary explained. "He had to teach her that she had to control her emotions and just be able to focus on making the correction and not get all flustered."

Bela realized it was impossible for Dominique to control her emotions all the time. "She is moody sometimes," he admitted, "but that makes her human."[4]

Bela wanted to motivate Dominique and muster her best effort. Sometimes that meant raising his voice. He would tell her she was not working hard enough or say that if she kept practicing like she was, she could expect to do poorly at the next meet. Usually, his tactics worked and Dominique improved.

"Sometimes it really gets her fired up and she tries harder," Kerri noted. "Other times her feelings get hurt and her attitude goes downhill."

Bela weighed his gymnasts periodically to make sure no one was gaining or losing too many pounds. He had a target weight for each gymnast. At four feet three inches and fifty-five pounds, Dominique was petite. While she was naturally slender, she had to be careful of what she ate. She tried to avoid sweets. She ate lots of vegetables and chicken, which were her favorites. When the team traveled for meets, Bela and his wife Marta, who coached alongside him, would suggest what foods were good for maximum performance. At first Dominique was nervous to eat in front of them, but she eventually got used to it.

Although workouts were intense, Bela encouraged parents to stay and watch their children practice. Whenever possible, Camelia would do so. She and the other onlookers peered through the glass as their children worked harder than most professional athletes. The parents could not hear Bela's comments, but they could tell from his facial expressions if their daughters were performing up to par or not. Occasionally, he closed off the viewing area so that no outsiders could distract his gymnasts from their training.

The Moceanus did not mind Bela's strictness. "Everything you do, if you want to reach perfection, you have to work hard," Camelia reasoned. "He makes her give 100% every day."[5]

Bela expected a lot from Dominique, and so did her parents.

"I thought maybe they did push her pretty hard, especially for being that young," Hilary admitted. "And also because she was moved into Bela's group, that made them realize she had potential. . . . I know that when she was younger she performed better when her parents weren't there because she didn't feel that extra added pressure."

While some thought Dominique's parents pushed her too much, Dimitry and Camelia saw things differently. They were supportive and wanted Dominique to be happy, but they also wanted to instill in her an appreciation for hard work.

"Gymnastics is a good sport to build character," Dimitry maintained. "And she'll have the character for the rest of her life." Dominique was proof of that principle: polite, well mannered, and a straight-A student at Bammel Middle School.

Dominique liked being at home with her parents, although she did not spend a lot of time there. Sunday was her only day off. She liked to unwind by playing Nintendo or computer games, reading books, or listening to music. Country music was her favorite; she especially liked Garth Brooks and Reba McEntire.

The Karolyi clan arrived in Columbus, Ohio, for the 1992 U.S. Championships ready to take the nation by storm. While Kim, Kerri, and Hilary were trying to make the Olympic team, Dominique was hoping to make the junior national team.

After checking into a hotel, the group began to get ready for an evening practice. Each gymnast had two sets of Karolyi warmups, a sort of uniform that they all wore to workouts.

"We usually all wore the same thing to practice so we'd look like a team," Hilary explained.

As they were getting ready for practice, someone asked, "So which warmups do you want to wear?"

"Warmups?" Dominique inquired innocently.

"Dominique, you brought your warmups, right?" her teammates asked.

"I didn't know which one to bring, and I think I forgot to bring both of them. I didn't bring any."

"Oh, no," her teammates lamented.

"She was so scared just because she didn't know what she was going to do," Hilary laughed. "It was cute. She ended up borrowing mine for the meet."

Despite the warmup-suit dilemma, Dominique did well in her first national competition, placing second after compulsories. In the few short months she had been with Karolyi's, her form had improved tremendously. Not only could she do the big skills, she was now learning to perfect them with style. In the optionals she edged out a talented field of juniors, including Amy Chow, Jennie Thompson, and former LaFleur's teammate Leila Pallardy, to place fifth. At age ten, Dominique became the youngest to ever qualify to the junior national team. On the individual apparatuses, she came in second on beam.

USA Gymnastics, the sport's governing body in the United States, awarded money to the athletes who made the national team, but by accepting the money an athlete forfeited her college eligibility. Dominique opted to accept the money she had won, thus becoming a professional.

For the first time, the media began to take notice of young Dominique. "Coming to this meet feels special because it's only us two little ones," she told reporters. "Everybody else is big out there. I feel like I'm a part of them now."

Jennie and Dominique were popular with the fans, who requested many autographs. It had only been six months since Dominique had switched to Karolyi's, and already she was attracting attention.

Bela talked about his two new stars on national television: "These two young ones—Jennie Thompson, who has already confirmed her national value at a few competitions, and the little Dominique Moceanu, the other one who is just coming up from the middle of nowhere—these names are going to be on from now on, and they're going to have to be strengthened and strengthened the closer we get to the Atlanta Olympic Games."

After the Championships, Dominique and her teammates did an exhibition at Rice University where she met Nadia Comaneci and Bart Conner for the first time. Dominique noticed her striking physical resemblance to Nadia while they were walking through an airport together. A traveller called out, "Nadia, your daughter looks exactly like you." Bela had noticed the same thing, and when he looked at Dominique he could not help but be reminded of the daring young pixie who had stolen the show at the Montreal Olympics in 1976.

"I can see in front of my eyes what I saw when Nadia was a little girl," he commented. "It's frighteningly similar."

Even Nadia could see the resemblance. "She looks like me," she admitted. "She's got a lot of similarities. She's got the face, the ponytail, the coach. I see myself in her."[6]

Dominique considered it a compliment when people told her how much she reminded them of Nadia. "Everybody says, 'Oh, gymnastics—Nadia,' " she observed. "They think about her. She's made history and we look alike, so it's really neat to be compared to her."

Dominique encouraged the comparison by wearing a ponytail bound with ribbons and straight bangs over her forehead. When she first watched videotapes from the 1976 Olympics, she thought, "Wow! We do look so much alike."[7]

"Physically, you can compare them," Bela said. "Many people say, 'Hey, the little Dominique looks like Nadia when she was thirteen-and-a-half.' Yes, that's true, no doubt about it. But personality-wise and temperament-wise they're totally different."

Nadia was quiet and reserved. Dominique, on the other hand, was easy to read. She did not hide her feelings. Bela could tell from her facial expressions what she was thinking. He found it easier to work with her because of these traits, likening her personality to that of Mary Lou Retton.

"Her personality came out right away from the first moment," Bela recalled, "her outgoing way of relating to everybody, and her smiling little face. So that was the first impression of her—a lovely, youth-ish personality—the one who really, really attached to my heart."

Dominique had the best of both worlds: the look of Nadia and the charm of Mary Lou.

The show at Rice University was followed by an autograph session for the fans, who brought articles of clothing, posters, and books to be signed. In assembly-line fashion, the autograph seekers moved down the table for each signature.

"We'd all just sign our names normally," Betty said. "But when Dominique starts signing her name, she put, 'Dominique, Atlanta Olympics, for sure.' I remember it because I think she passed it down to me after she signed it. I was reading it and I couldn't believe it. Then Marta and Bela came over. They were just laughing. It was funny."

"There she comes, Dominique Moceanu," Bela remembered with a smile, "and when the little paper of the people gets to her, she signs 'Dominique Moceanu, Olympic All-Around Champion, Atlanta 1996, for sure.' "

"Well, I was only ten when I went to my first exhibition, and I didn't know any better," Dominique explained years later, rolling her eyes with embarrassment. "Everybody was like, 'Oh, are you going to go to the Olympics?' And I was like, 'I hope so. Yeah.' So I wrote, '1996 Olympics, for sure.' "

After the exhibition, Dominique and her teammates enjoyed a break from the gym. Bela usually let his students take a week or two off in the summer to relax and rest some of their injuries after the competitive season ended. Dominique had been experiencing pain in her wrist and welcomed the respite.

For vacation, Dominique, her mom, and her sister went back to Tampa since Dimitry was still living there. While in town, Dominique visited LaFleur's and her old teammates. She told everyone about Karolyi's, how hard it was, and how much she was learning. She also had some interesting things to say about her new coach.

"She said [Bela] was really mean and that he made fun of her," Shelly Cavaliere remembered. "[He said] that her butt was like a hot air balloon and they needed to pop it."

His comments sometimes seemed unnecessarily cruel, but Dominique realized Bela's insults were intended to make her tougher and motivate her to improve. While such a coaching style was not effective with every athlete, many gymnasts who had been successful under Bela recognized his tremendous abilities and could tolerate, if not completely excuse, his harsh words.

"At first when he came to this country he didn't have a good grasp of the English language," Hilary explained. "When he got upset or angry he'd just say stuff. . . . He'll call you stupid every once in a while if you can't get a trick, and if he thinks you're overweight he'll call you something to do with that." But Hilary was quick to point out his strengths. "Bela's a really good coach and he's a really good person, too. He builds good relationships with his gymnasts even though he's tough. We respect him and we like him."

In July, Kim, Betty, and Kerri all left for the 1992 Olympics in Barcelona, Spain. Hilary just missed making the team due to a shoulder injury. Dominique watched the Games on television and yearned for her chance to represent the United States of America at the Olympics. Kim was favored to win the competition but fell on balance beam in the team compulsories and stepped out of bounds on floor during the all-around to finish tenth.

Bela attributed Kim's dismal performance to a lack of support from American judges, beginning with the U.S. Championships and Olympic Trials. He had felt betrayed by the team selection process which had ranked Shannon Miller higher than Kim even though Shannon had not scored as many points as Kim. At the conclusion of the Games, Bela stormed over to one of the American judges and gave her a piece of his mind. He questioned her patriotism and likened her to a piece of garbage. So discouraged by the outcome of these Olympics, he unexpectedly announced his retirement following the team competition.

"In the end, the 1992 Olympic Games left a bitter taste in my mouth that I could no longer swallow," Bela later explained. "It was everything in combination—the judging, the cheating, the Nationals and Trials, the media's method of pushing the sport in the wrong direction, the [U.S. gymnastics] federation's apathy, and the little victims. . . . After the 1992 Games, I looked around and saw that my frustrations were no longer worth the effort. For the first time I felt an emptiness that could not be filled by returning to the gym to coach the next generation of elite gymnasts."[8]

At her home in Houston, Dominique was shocked by the news of Bela's retirement. She wondered if he was serious, and if so, who would continue to train her.

She and her parents were also upset by how the media

represented gymnastics during and after the Olympics. Kim was featured on the cover of *Newsweek* magazine immediately following the Games wearing a look of deep concentration while wiping chalk off her mouth. The caption read, "It Hurts—Do We Push Teen Athletes Too Hard?" The *Newsweek* article bluntly stated that young bodies were not meant to endure the stress to the joints inflicted by the intense training of elite-level gymnastics. It described the obsession of some parents with the success of their children and claimed that focusing on maintaining low body fat and weight was unhealthy and could lead to eating disorders. A photograph of Dominique chalking up next to Hilary, Kim, and Kerri also appeared in the piece.

The article angered Dominique's parents. They felt it was an unfair representation of the sport and bristled at the assertion that elite-level gymnastics was unhealthy. Besides, they liked the discipline Dominique was learning as a gymnast.

"It depends on the support of the family," Dimitry countered. "Is it better to leave them alone on the street corner, hanging around, watching TV, drinking, smoking? It's better for them to do something with their lives, to prepare for their lives."[9]

Not everyone shared the Moceanus' view. Steve Jacobson, a *Newsday* sports columnist, said of elite gymnasts, "Their whole lives have been dwarfed and warped. Their bodies have been kept deliberately small and immature, because by the time a girl begins to mature into a young woman, her body type changes and she can't do the mechanical things."

Aric Press, who had written parts of the infamous *Newsweek* article, said in an interview, "I'm afraid it comes down to sexism. What's all right for little boys to do in certain circumstances, evidently is not all right for little girls."

Sadly, the article started a media crusade against women's gymnastics. More newspaper and magazine articles began cropping up, followed by television talk shows that interrogated former national gymnasts and news programs that questioned the sport's legitimacy. The furor culminated in a scathing book entitled <u>Little Girls in Pretty Boxes</u> which presented a one-sided view that likened elite-level gymnastics and figure skating to child abuse.

"[The upcoming stars] embody the unspoken imperative of elite figure skating and gymnastics: keep them coming, and keep them young, small and more dazzling than the ones we already have," wrote Joan Ryan, the author of the book. "The national appetite for new stars is insatiable. Deep down, we know that our consumption and disposal of these young athletes are tantamount to child exploitation and, in too many cases, child abuse."[10]

The book enraged both the gymnastics and figure skating communities. Bela, who was one of the biggest targets of the book, claimed it was trash.

"What a sorry way to make a living," he retorted. "She has no business analyzing the work of someone who has put his whole life, heart, and integrity into this sport. . . . To take that pride away, it's a crime. This woman should be ashamed of herself."[11]

"There's been different things said of Bela's gym and the handling of the athletes," James said. "The coaches, I believe, are doing what the athletes want done in that gym and what the parents want done. I watched Bela through the eleven years that I worked for him. I watched him through Mary Lou, Phoebe Mills, Dianne Durham, Kim Zmeskal, and now with Dominique. Bela is a good coach because he can sense personalities and he can work with each individual according to that individual. Some people need a kick in the butt, so you give it to them; some people need a pat on the back on a bad day. Dominique is not going to take a pat on the back at the end of the day when she knows she's done a bad job. Period. It just isn't going to happen, because she's going to be frustrated with herself and she's going to realize, 'Hey, this guy's giving me a bunch of bull.' "

After several obligatory tours with his Olympic gymnasts, Bela retreated from the nagging press to his fifty-five-acre spread in the Sam Houston National Forest outside Houston.

"Both of us, myself and my wife, we decided to go into a different stage," Bela said while relaxing at his ranch. "That doesn't mean quite a retirement like most of the other people would understand, but retirement from coaching national team gymnasts for the national team."

As Bela bowed out, Achim Fassbender stepped up to fill the master's shoes. Achim was a German who had migrated to the U.S. in 1981 and had worked for two years with the women's gymnastics team at the University of Kentucky. A controversial character, he had once described collegiate gymnastics as ridiculous and admitted he would have liked to see the gymnastics scholarship money spent on improving the school instead of the athletics. After coaching at Bela's summer camps for many years, he had begun working permanently for Bela in May 1992.

With Bela's departure and the usual letdown that followed the Olympics, many veteran gymnasts departed. Betty retired and went home to Illinois to finish her last two years of high school. Kerri left and went to Brown's Gymnastics, but she was there only a couple of months because the head coaches, Kevin and Rita Brown, divorced. Kerri then went to Dynamo Gymnastics to train with Steve Nunno. Kim and Hilary stayed at Karolyi's to keep in shape for professional tours but came into the gym only in the evenings.

Dominique and Jennie were now the best in the gym. These two tiny titans had to carry the weight of the Karolyi reputation on their narrow shoulders. In early December, they traveled to

São Paulo, Brazil, for the 1992 Junior Pan American Championships. This was Dominique's first international gymnastics meet and first overseas trip since the age of four when the Moceanus had taken a six-week tour of Europe.

Competing in the youth (children's) division, Jennie and Dominique performed well under the pressure. The two comprised the entire U.S. team in their division. A squad usually included three athletes, which allowed the lowest score on each event to be dropped. With only two entries, the U.S. did not have this luxury. Despite the disadvantage, Jennie and Dominique soundly beat Canada for the top position. They were a one-two punch, finishing first and second, respectively. The next day, Dominique nearly swept the event finals, winning vault, bars, and floor.

Dominique liked Brazil, although she found it difficult to communicate with the natives since she did not speak Portuguese. She also found the political unrest in the city unsettling. Guards with guns were everywhere. For the most part, Dominique and Jennie stayed at the gym or in their hotel, where they ate most of their meals.

"The food was really good," Dominique said. "They had rice and this meat stuff."[12]

The other gymnasts felt differently about their meals. "The meat was like dog meat," one parent traveling with the gymnasts observed. "It was nasty tasting. My daughter wouldn't eat it; she's spoiled. Dominique thought it was great and ate it."

Although she was generally easy to please, Dominique did admit that the pizza "was sick. Me and Jen were about to barf."

Following their success at the Pan Am Games, Dominique and Jennie found themselves on the cover of the February 1993 issue of *International Gymnast* magazine in which they were touted as the future hope of the American team. Dominique was thrilled to be on the cover. Her parents had it framed, and she hung it in her bedroom. She and Jennie were also featured in the "Faces in the Crowd" section of *Sports Illustrated* magazine and awarded engraved sterling silver bowls for being selected to appear in the piece.

After being at Karolyi's for little more than a year, Dominique was already being asked to sign autographs and had appeared on national television and on the cover of a prestigious gymnastics magazine. Everything was going according to plan, except for one problem: Bela was no longer her coach. She hoped that somehow he would change his mind about retiring.

Chapter 4

Building

A chim was as strict as ever after Dominique and Jennie's victories in Brazil. He did not let his athletes savor their success; otherwise, they might slack off. Achim demanded perfection. During practice he could be heard barking orders and bragging about the discipline he intended to instill in his pupils. Although his accent resembled Bela's, he was unable to motivate his gymnasts the way Bela had.

No one believed that Bela could avoid elite-level gymnastics for long, but 1993 had already begun and there was still no sign of him. Marta, however, was coaching in the evenings.

Dominique was improving steadily, but she still needed more consistency. She pushed herself to go to the gym, even when her body ached so badly she could barely move. She suffered from a touch of tendinitis in her knee that never seemed to heal and growth plate problems in her wrists. Stiffness in her hamstrings was bothersome as well. In addition, new injuries began to crop up.

"I developed a problem with the middle toe on my left foot," Dominique said. "The skin underneath it cracked and split from the pressure of my routine. Since I worked out every day, it could never heal. . . . Each time I got on the beam, my toe began killing me. Finally it became so painful that I couldn't ignore it. As soon as I started wearing beam shoes, it made all the difference. My toe healed."[1]

Although she had a handful of irritating injuries, she was thankful she had never suffered something more serious like a broken bone.

One of her first meets of the 1993 season was the Karolyi's Invitational. Dominique won the event, edging out teammates Monica and Jennie. In March she participated in the American Classic. She placed a disappointing tenth in the junior division with a total of 36.00 points but still managed to qualify to the 1993 U.S. Championships.

As winter turned to spring, Bela finally awoke from hibernation. He put away his cowboy boots and jeans and dusted off his tennis shoes and warmup suit. It was time to do a little coaching. He accompanied his past and future stars on the 1993 Gold Gymnastics Tour from April to June. Dominique and Jennie traveled with Kim, Betty, and Hilary. The five of them even performed a dance routine together. Jennie was injured and did not perform on any events, but Dominique impressed the enthusiastic crowds with her bar and floor sets. She enjoyed being with her older teammates and under Bela's direction once again, even if only for a short time.

When the performances ended for the evening, Dominique goofed around with her teammates in the hotel. "We got into trouble a lot," Betty laughed. "Me and Kim were the instigators, and Jennie and Dominique—maybe because they were younger—looked up to us and wanted to copy us. We did what kids do—stupid things. We ran around the halls and played on the elevators. We played little jokes and pranks. We dropped pennies from the balcony and tried to hit people. Bela caught us a number of times then yelled at us and said we were a bad influence on Jennie and Dominique because we would always get them into trouble."

Bela was strict on trips. He did not allow his gymnasts to leave their rooms at night to roam the halls. He was responsible for their well being and did not want anything bad to happen to them.

Dominique and Nadia became close friends on the tour. Although Nadia was sometimes mistaken for Dominique's mother, she was like a big sister or mentor who understood what her young friend was going through. Dominique frequently asked Nadia for advice. Since she spoke Romanian, she sometimes talked with Nadia in her native language. At first she was hesitant, but as she got to know Nadia better she felt more comfortable conversing in this way. Occasionally, the two were joined in conversation by Bela, Marta, and Betty, who also spoke Romanian.

"Sometimes they speak in Romanian, which can make you feel like the foreigner in the group," Kim laughed. "It's kind of strange. Sometimes when we travel I think they forget that I'm along and I don't understand what they're talking about."

Since Dominique understood the Karolyi's native tongue, Bela and Marta spoke in Hungarian when they wanted to speak privately. This may have been an unnecessary precaution because, as Bela joked, "Her Romanian is worse than my English."

Besides touring, Dominique, Jennie, Kim, Bart, and Nadia visited the Bart Conner Gymnastics Academy in Norman, Oklahoma, for an *International Gymnast* Back-to-School Fashion Collection photo shoot. Dominique enjoyed posing in different leotards donated by various manufacturers. The layout was well received in the August/September and October issues of *IG*.

While the tour and fashion shoot were fun, Dominique was glad to be back home with her family in mid-June. Her dad had finally sold his car dealership in Tampa and joined the family in Houston. For the past year-and-a-half, Dimitry had been commuting on weekends between the two cities. Now the family was together for good, and Dominique was glad. Dimitry took a job with a Ford car dealership as a sales manager, and shortly after he arrived in Houston the Moceanus moved out of Bela's rental house to their own home about a mile from the gym and one street over from the Zmeskals.

Dominique was home only briefly before going to Bela's ranch to train for the remainder of the summer. The ranch, located an hour outside Houston in the middle of the Sam Houston National Forest, was the site of Bela's summer camps. Campers enjoyed a rustic setting and accommodations in air-conditioned cedar log cabins. There were two main gyms, one for the campers and one for the elites. Posters of famous gymnasts hung on the wooden walls of the elite gym. One side was equipped with a couple sets of uneven bars and a row of four balance beams—one for each elite training at the camp—while the other side sported a light-blue floor exercise mat and a vault and tumble-track in opposite corners.

Bela sometimes allowed small groups of campers into the gym to watch him coach his top kids. As long as they were quiet, they could observe Dominique and Jennie practicing. Some campers even got to meet Dominique between workouts and at camp activities, which included horseback riding, basketball, tennis, and volleyball. A pool and a lake on the grounds also accommodated one of Dominique's favorite activities, swimming.

Shortly after summer training began, Jennie left Karolyi's and went to Dynamo Gymnastics, where reigning World Champion Shannon Miller trained. Since Bela was not coaching her consistently, she felt she would be better off working with Dynamo head coach Steve Nunno. She was familiar with his coaching because she had trained with him earlier in her gymnastics career.

With Championships only a few weeks away, Monica also left to continue training with Achim, who had taken a coaching job at nearby Culhane Gymnastics. Russ Ward assumed the vacated head-coaching position. Coaches did not last long in the Karolyi camp. They frequently quit or were fired. As Bela had high expectations for his athletes, he also had high standards for his coaches.

There had always been a little tension between Monica and Dominique, especially when Jennie was injured and Monica took her place at a competition. "She'd make me feel down," Monica admitted about Dominique. "Whenever I'd start doing well she'd be like, 'Well, you know I'm better than you. You don't deserve to go on this with me. Jennie better get well.'

"She didn't like it that me and Jennie were such good friends. I had given Jennie a best-friend charm for her birthday, and two days later Dominique came in with a *huge* one and gave it to Jennie, too. Jennie was like, 'Oh gosh, now what am I supposed to do?' "

In the gym, Monica never seemed to get the attention Dominique and Jennie did. The coaches picked the pair out of the group and worked almost exclusively with them. They made occasional comments to the other athletes when they were doing something wrong, but for the most part they focused on the two stars.

"They'd have like three private lessons a week," Monica claimed. "I was lucky if I got in one. They never seemed to have enough time for me. I think they were told who to work with by Bela and Marta. I felt like I was being held back. I was never pushed to my full potential. I never got to try things."

Without any teammates, Dominique now had to push herself. "I feel bad for Dominique . . . [but] she's adjusted well working by herself," Kim said. "That's what was really good about Jennie and her—they really pushed each other."

With everyone else gone, Dominique sometimes doubted her decision to stay. She did not think Bela was serious about his retirement, yet he showed no signs of changing his mind.

"I kept working on my routines and prayed he would come back," she said. "I knew gymnastics was his life. But he stayed out for a long time and I began to wonder."

Pushing her misgivings to the back of her mind, she prepared for the 1993 Sports Festival. It took some time to get used to her new coach, but Dominique's easygoing personality helped. At the end of July, she left for San Antonio, Texas, the site of the competition. The Festival was unique because it involved many Olympic sports, such as track and field, swimming, and diving. Phoebe Mills, a former Karolyi student and 1988 Olympic bronze medalist on the balance beam, was competing as a diver. She finished seventh in the ten-meter platform.

Dominique enjoyed meeting the other athletes. Despite being the shortest at the Festival, she drew a lot of attention to herself during an open workout when she and gymnast Tom Meadows from the University of Oklahoma performed their rendition of the rap song *"Baby Got Back"* by Sir Mix-a-Lot.

Dominique performed solidly in the all-around meet and placed twelfth. At the conclusion of the competition, Bart Conner remarked, "Of course, you know what happened when Bela Karolyi trained a Romanian many years ago, Nadia Comaneci. He produced the greatest gymnast of all time, so we may be looking at a future superstar."

Although Shannon Miller was the star of the meet, Dominique received her fair share of attention. During event finals, the crowd erupted in applause every time she landed a pass while warming up her tumbling on floor. When she finished her routine, a score of 9.60 was flashed on the scoreboard. She was not thrilled. Neither were the 13,000 fans, who began to boo. The score was later adjusted upward to a 9.65, but it was still only good enough for fourth place.

Dominique used the exact same floor music—and almost the same tumbling—that Kim had used to win the 1991 World Championships. Kim said, "I remember her calling me into the gym one day and saying, 'Guess what music I got? Guess what music? I got your music!' "

Kim normally trained in the afternoons for exhibitions. When she and Dominique practiced the dance parts of their floor routines, they played *"In the Mood"* while each simultaneously performed her own version of the routine. They joked that they should do it in an exhibition sometime, although they would have to draw straws to determine which one had to do the tumbling.

Watching Dominique perform to her old music took some getting used to for Kim. "That was a little strange at first," she said. "Betty called me and she was like, 'Can you believe she's doing that?' And I said, 'Well, it's an honor for me for her to be using it.' She danced it really well and it showed her personality."

"Her idol was Kim," choreographer Geza Pozsar explained.

"She really wanted to do that piece. I tried to tell her, 'Listen, this is Kim's music,' but . . . she loved it. I was against it because it was already used, but she insisted on it. She's pretty stubborn."

In early August, Dominique participated in the 1993 U.S. Classic in Austin, Texas. She did not do as well as usual, placing eighth overall in the junior division. Fatigue from touring all spring and competing all summer was taking its toll, but she could not rest until after the 1993 Junior National Championships in Salt Lake City, her biggest meet of the year. She had a solid meet and placed seventh, while her former teammate Jennie won the competition.

Following the Championships, Dominique took a much-needed break from gymnastics. But after only a week off, it was back to the daily grind. The school year began and she returned to the gym to learn new skills and routines for the upcoming season. Bela went back into hibernation and Dominique was left to motivate herself.

In late October, she traveled to Charleroi, Belgium, for a prestigious competition: the 1993 International Tournament of Junior Women's Gymnastics. She competed against some of the top juniors from Romania, western Europe, and the Ukraine, outdoing one of the best Romanians, Alexandra Marinescu, to place fifth. Dominique sparkled in the event finals, winning gold on beam and bronze on bars.

The American Classic was held March 1994 in Orlando, Florida. Dominique did well in compulsories but had falls on bars and floor in optionals. She placed fourth in the all-around.

Training was grueling and tedious, but Dominique was improving. She nearly had the coaches' undivided attention since only she and April Burkholder, an upcoming elite hoping to make the 2000 Olympics, were in the group. It had only been a little over two years since Dominique had first arrived at Karolyi's, and now she was the top athlete in his gym and the only one left of her original junior elite squad. All the others had either switched gyms or quit.

The month of May brought an end to Bela's self-imposed exile. At the halfway mark between two Olympiads, Bela announced he was coming out of retirement to coach Kim Zmeskal as she tried for the 1996 Games.

"That was the moment when I said, 'Well, just forget everything else—there is no more place to run,' " he stated. " 'It's worth it to do it. It's worth it for the kids. It's worth it for the general idea of the Olympic Games.' And I said, 'Let's do it. And if I'm doing it, let's do it right.' "

Bela said he would not have come out of retirement for anyone but Kim, who was surprised by her strong desire to return to gymnastics. "I didn't even think I'd want to do gymnastics after the Olympics," she said. "I was thinking, 'I'll do the nine or so exhibitions that we have to do afterwards, then I'm going to go back to school, finish high school, go to college'—just like that. It took me about three or four months, then I was like, 'I miss gymnastics.'

"I had been struggling with wanting to start training again for a really long time. I wanted to train for '93 Worlds, and Bela was going to work with me on that. That kind of faded away because I started listening to everybody else who was telling me I was missing out on all these great things . . . so I decided I didn't want to waste another year."

But Kim had become dissatisfied with merely performing at exhibitions and overly critical of herself for mistakes made during her performances. Bela had told her, "Don't worry about it; it's just a show," but he had sensed she still hungered for competition.

Kim admitted, "I remember spending many nights crying with Hilary Grivich here at my house, going, 'I don't know what I should do. Should I tell him? Or should I not say anything?' I thought I was being kind of foolish in thinking that I could still do this again."

After one particular exhibition, while sitting in an airport, Bela had turned to Kim and asked if she wanted to compete again. Relieved, Kim had explained her feelings, and the decision to make another run for the Olympics had been made.

Upon his reemergence on the competitive gymnastics scene, Bela decided to beef up his coaching staff. Coincidentally, Alexander Alexandrov, the former head coach of women's gymnastics in the Soviet Union, was looking for work in the United States, so Bela hired him. Although the two had been enemies in the past, they put aside their differences to train Bela's top athletes.

They made a powerful and experienced team. Alexander got to work right away on Dominique's weaknesses. He stretched her splits to enhance her flexibility, paid close attention to her form, and made her do countless repetitions on each apparatus to improve her consistency. His goal was for Dominique to become the junior national champion later that summer at the U.S. Championships.

Kim suffered a serious setback to her Olympic dream in June when she tore a ligament in her knee on a double back flip. While recuperating from surgery, she could do little more than light conditioning. Still, Kim did not miss a practice, even though Bela only came into the gym sporadically.

By the time the U.S. Championships began in Nashville, Dominique's hard work and attention to detail appeared to be paying off. She was in top shape and comfortable with her routines. She began the competition with solid and consistent compulsory sets that all earned scores in the 9.45 to 9.50 range. After the first day, she held a large lead over the nearest competitor, Doni Thompson from the Colorado Aerials.

Dominique was determined to maintain her lead, and on August 25 she began her quest to become the best junior in America. Her first event was the treacherous balance beam, and she was last up. Unfortunately, on her first trick, a front flip mount, she was a little crooked and fell off the side. Unfazed, she jumped back on the beam and continued, nailing three consecutive layouts, a front flip, and a back handspring with a quarter twist. She finished with a stuck double back dismount and sheepishly walked over to her coaches knowing the fall could cost her the championship. Bela had not made the trip to Nashville, but Alexander, who was there in his place, was not pleased. The score was a dismal 9.20.

Dominique rebounded on floor by hitting all her passes, including a clean double layout and a Rudi. But she made a beginner's mistake, stepping out of bounds *before* her first tumbling pass. She earned a 9.60.

In a freak accident on her initial vault, Dominique's hands slid off the horse. She flipped uncontrollably through the air and landed hard on the mat. Fortunately, she was not hurt, and she opted to take her second vault. The best of two scores would be used. Her heart pounding, she stepped up to her starting marker for another try, determined not to make the same mistake again. A few gymnasts had become seriously injured—in some cases paralyzed—from botched roundoff-entry vaults. One gymnast, Julissa Gomez, had even died from a vaulting injury. Dominique pushed these thoughts from her mind and concentrated on making the necessary correction.

When given the signal, she ran down the runway, hit the

springboard squarely, and flew backwards to the horse. This time her hands found the padded vault and pushed off strongly. She twisted and flipped flawlessly, then landed with ease. After flashing a smile of relief to the judges, she walked off the mat thankful to have escaped without any further problems. The second vault earned a 9.725.

On bars, her last event, Dominique smoothly caught both release moves, a Gienger and a Tkatchev. The highlight of her set was a textbook-perfect double layout flyaway. Dominique was met with big hugs from her coaches, and she pumped her fists excitedly. She knew she had done it. Her score of 9.50 was good enough to capture her first national title.

Dominique shined in the event finals, winning vault and floor and placing third on bars and beam. The next day she sat between Kim and Betty to watch the seniors' competition. She saw her former teammate Jennie place fourth and witnessed the remarkable performances of Dominique Dawes, who won the all-around over Shannon Miller and went on to sweep all four event finals. Dominique longed to compete against the older athletes but was pleased with the status of being the best junior in the country.

When Dominique received *International Gymnast* magazine in the mail the next month, she found herself on the cover along with Dominique Dawes and a caption that read "The Dominique Duo!" She was definitely making a splash in the gymnastics community.

Everything was going quite well. Besides winning a big meet and being on the cover of a magazine, her father finally allowed her to get her ears double pierced for her thirteenth birthday. Some girls might have begun bothering their parents about dating after becoming teenagers, but Dominique knew it was out of the question, especially with her overprotective father.

"Don't even get me started," she moaned to a reporter while rolling her eyes. "My mom's a little better. But mention anything about boys, and my dad goes crazy."[2]

Shortly after the Championships, a famous elite with a sparkling résumé was added to the Karolyi roster: Svetlana Boginskaya. Svetlana, the 1989 World Champion from Belarus, decided to make a comeback and began training with Bela. She chose him partly because of his claim after Kim's victory at the 1991 World Championships that Svetlana's time was over. The statement had so infuriated her that she felt compelled to prove him wrong.

Bela, however, was hesitant to coach her, given the controversial history between her and Kim. "Everything about her was negative," he maintained. "I thought she was the most arrogant, most impossible person I ever saw. I thought she had a nasty personality. Everything I saw from her on the floor was bad: the way she treated people, the way she talked with coaches and teammates, the way she scared the athletes from other teams."

Indeed, under the old Soviet system, Svetlana had not been very nice. She admitted she had tried to intimidate the other competitors by glaring at them and never smiling. She had been unhappy and pressured into continuing with her career despite wanting to retire. As a young girl she had sometimes bitten and kicked other gymnasts whom she thought were better than her. The parents of the other children had bribed her to be nice with candy. She had accepted the bribe yet continued to pester the other girls.

But Svetlana had changed since moving to the United States in February 1994. With her teeth newly capped, she enjoyed smiling frequently. While watching the 1994 World Championships on television, she had decided to contact Bela because she still wanted to do gymnastics—this time for herself and her love of the sport.

Bela found he was pleasantly surprised by Svetlana's personality. "After what I used to see in her," he said, "you cannot imagine how surprised I was when she comes down here and she is one of the sweetest people I've ever known. She never complains, never treats people bad, and is the hardest worker we have. I always thought I was pretty good at knowing people's personalities. But this was one of the greatest mistakes I've made."[3]

"I'm the happiest person in the world," an Americanized Svetlana gushed, "because I have the chance to be here and to work out with the best coaches in the world."

Along with Svetlana, Jennie Thompson rejoined the group. Since Bela was coaching again, she abruptly moved back to Houston. The Thompsons had been split between Texas and Oklahoma, and Jennie's mom Samm had wanted the family to be together again. It had been a strain to have her husband in Houston and the rest of the family in Oklahoma City. Besides, Jennie's brother had been miserable.

"I moved back because my brother was unhappy where he was living," Jennie said. "He liked living in Houston."

Bela thought that having two veterans in the group—Kim and Svetlana—made for an ideal training situation. "We are shooting for something that the gymnastics sport needs," he commented. "To see their idols, the great stars, back performing."

"I look up to them a lot," Dominique said of her veteran teammates. "They're really good. And it's good that they keep on doing it as long as they like it."

Since May, Dominique's group had more than doubled in size and reputation. Dominique and Jennie's training rivalry picked up right where it had left off. Kim and Svetlana, once cast as enemies by the media, found themselves becoming friends.

"It's just something that I've always dreamed of happening, of being able to be friends with her in an everyday situation," Kim admitted. "It's been good. I think a lot of the stuff between Svetlana and me was built up higher than it really was."

Svetlana attributed their former rivalry to the cold war: "I was Russian; she was American. We were competitive."

"To have Svetlana here, I would never have dreamed that that would have happened," Kim added. "But it's been really good for both of us. We're going through essentially the same things—having to come back after not training for a long period of time."

With so many potential 1996 Olympians in the gym, it was just like old times. Bela was excited about the possibility of having up to half of the U.S. Olympic team and one member of the Belorussian team all from his club.

As practice became more intense, Dominique and her family decided it would be best for her to change schools. She enrolled at Northland Christian, a private school a couple of miles from the gym that accommodated the Karolyi's workout schedule. Dominique enjoyed the school and her classmates.

"We want them to respect Christianity and those beliefs," noted her school counselor Deanna Graves, "and what we're hoping to help kids develop into are strong Christian leaders. They come from many different denominations and have different faiths."

As long as the athletes took a Bible class, they were allowed to attend only a few hours of school each day. Dominique's favorite subjects were spelling and history. Her least favorite was math, which she found the most challenging. She took three classes each semester the first year—pre-algebra, English, and earth science—plus Bible, which she learned on an independent-study basis because the timing of the class did not fit into her schedule.

Dominique was a diligent and reliable student. In the eighth grade she received mostly Bs—commendable grades considering she had to juggle school, workouts, and competitions. When she traveled, she tried to get her assignments before she left so there would not be such a big pile of schoolwork when she returned.

"She worked really hard for her grades," Deanna said. "Some students can pick things up very, very easily. I think she is a strong student, but I think she had to put effort into her schoolwork just like she does into her gymnastics."

In early October, Dominique and her teammates flew to Mexico City for the "Espectaculo Gimnasio Milo 94," a show organized by the International Management Group and Paul Ziert. Two top Romanians, Lavinia Milosovici and Gina Gogean, also participated in the two-day exhibition.

Dominique performed beautifully on the unevens, soaring high above the bar on both her release moves. Young gymnasts from Bart Conner's Gymnastics Academy, who were also part of the exhibition, stood by the bars in rapt attention as the routine unfolded before their wondering eyes.

Between shows, Dominique and her teammates went shopping. They enjoyed visiting colorful merchandise displays along the sidewalk and charming boutiques filled with exotic jewelry. At a sporting goods store in a local mall they participated in a press conference and autograph session. In addition, Bela hosted a clinic for the Mexican gymnasts. Dominique, Betty, Kim, Jennie, and Svetlana demonstrated how to properly execute the basic skills in gymnastics, then the locals had their chance to try a few things under Bela's guidance.

The Team World Championships took place in Germany in

November. Since Dominique was not old enough to compete, she watched the meet on television. A gymnast had to turn fifteen in the year of the World Championships to be eligible to compete, and Dominique was only thirteen. However, she would be able to compete in the 1995 World Championships since athletes who were eligible for the '96 Olympics were also allowed to compete at the '95 Worlds.

The U.S. team did well, placing second behind Romania. It was hard for Dominique to merely watch the meet; she wanted to be on the floor representing her country.

The past year had been a time of laying the groundwork for the future. Dominique had competed in a few big meets and had been on national television a handful of times. Anxious to face the best the United States and the world had to offer, she looked forward to the upcoming year where she would make her debut in the senior division.

Dominique enjoyed privileges that few other gymnasts had ever had: the opportunity to train under the direction of the top two gymnastics coaches and alongside two world champions. She also had a gymnast her age to compete against daily in the gym. If she could capitalize on these advantages, she would be poised to win many accolades in the coming year.

Chapter 5

Stepping into the Spotlight

The new year began with a bang. Dominique and Jennie were pictured on the cover of the January 1995 issue of *Sports Illustrated for Kids* and touted as future Olympians. But shortly after the article was run, Jennie began experiencing problems in the gym. A constant pain in her elbow made practice very difficult.

Eventually, the stress in the gym became too much for her. Samm, her mother, came home from work one day to find Jennie lying in bed buried under her covers. Sobbing uncontrollably, she said she never wanted to go back to Karolyi's. If she were going to do gymnastics at all, she wanted to do it at Dynamo.

When Jennie had come back to Houston from Oklahoma City several months earlier, her mother had believed she would be fine at either gym. But Samm now realized her daughter liked the coaches at Dynamo better. Steve Nunno was strict but not as tough as Bela.

"Jennie has always had a connection with Steve, and we didn't even ask her how she felt about moving back to Houston," Samm confessed. "She and Steve just have a special relationship. Sometimes I think she tells him more than she tells me."

Jennie was allowed to return to Oklahoma City, but she had to go alone and stay with another family. Her mother insisted the rest of the Thompsons remain together in Houston. Regrettably, soon after her arrival at Dynamo, Jennie had to have surgery on her left arm to remove bone chips before she could resume full training. After the procedure, she found she was still struggling in the gym.

Her parents decided enough was enough. Samm went to Oklahoma to bring Jennie home, insisting that she quit. "When we told her she was quitting, she was just miserable," her mother said. "With Jennie, it's either her way, or it isn't."[1]

But Jennie had other plans. After a tearful argument, she convinced Samm to let her remain in gymnastics. She also persuaded her mother to move back to Oklahoma. Happily, the new arrangement worked well, and at last Jennie began to improve.

Back in Houston, Dominique had again lost her friend and training rival. As before, she was forced to rely on herself for motivation to keep improving in the gym.

Dominique's first competition of the new year was the Reese's Cup held January 1995 in Portland, Oregon. This was a professional meet in which the participants used costumes and music on bars, beam, and floor. The vault was the only apparatus omitted. On her first event, Dominique, attired in a black feline costume complete with ears and whiskers, slinked up to the low bar as—appropriately—*"Black Cat"* by Janet Jackson blared from the loudspeakers. She swung and flipped with the greatest of ease, purring her way to a first place finish.

In a different outfit, four-foot-five sixty-six-pound Dominique was vibrant on beam, placing third. On floor, wearing a short white skirt with red polka dots over her leotard, she thrilled the crowd with a new, energetic routine to *"Let's Twist Again."* She clapped, hopped, and played air piano during her set.

Dominique's floor routine was only a month old. Geza Pozsar had come up with the idea for the music while watching an ice-skating exhibition.

"I saw Oksana Baiul and Viktor Petrenko on TV doing a mixed pair singing *'Let's Twist Again,'* " he explained. "It looked so funny and the people got so excited about it, so I talked to Barry about using the same music."

Barry Nease, who composed pieces for all the top U.S. gymnasts, had liked the idea as well. The minute-and-a-half composition which was properly called *"La Paloma Twist"* had taken him over sixty hours to arrange in his Colorado studio using a computerized orchestra he called "virtual music." Normally this arrangement would have cost $200, but Barry was one of Dominique's sponsors and did not charge her.

The final version of the music had been selected jointly by Barry and Geza with input from Dominique and Bela. "He has really good ideas," Barry said of Bela. "He's wonderful to work with and very supportive."

"Dominique is a very, very important factor," Geza added. "You have to like the music. You're not going to want to do something you hate."

The debut of Dominique's new set was a success. She came in fourth, winning a total of $3,600 in prize money.

"I like to compete like this," she said. "It's really fun. The audience loves this stuff."

The audience got another chance to see her at the 1995 American Classic held February 16-17 in Oakland, California. This meet re-ranked the gymnasts for the upcoming year. Entering the senior division for the first time, Dominique faced her first real head-to-head match-up against two-time World Champion Shannon Miller. Dominique had competed against Shannon once before at the 1993 Sports Festival, but then—at the age of eleven—her career had only just begun.

In the compulsory round, Dominique was fantastic. She and Shannon tied with the highest scores on beam and floor. By the end of the evening, she was trailing Shannon by less than two tenths.

Dominique was even more impressive the next day in optionals with a 9.95 on her one-and-a-half-twisting Yurchenko vault for the top score of the day. She had some problems on bars, scoring a low 9.275, but she rebounded on beam and floor to score a 9.70 and 9.625, respectively. Shannon was nearly flawless on each event and captured the victory, with Dominique and Amanda Borden tying for second.

At the press conference after the meet, Dominique said, "I have been working very hard in the gym, but I could have done a lot better. Now I need to go back to the gym and learn some new optional skills."

Her second-place finish qualified her to the Pan American Games held in Mar del Plata, Argentina. However, she sustained an ankle injury shortly after returning home and had to withdraw from both the American Cup and the Pan Am Games.

After missing all the competitions in March, Dominique was anxious to get back into action. On April 5 she participated in an exhibition at the Spectrum in Philadelphia called "Superstars of

Gymnastics." The show began with a dramatic introduction of each athlete complete with spotlights and music. As the announcer boomed her name over the loudspeakers, Dominique circled the high bar a few times then dismounted with a double layout flyaway. The crowd roared as she landed with a smile and a wave.

Her first performance of the night was on floor. The routine was solid but lacked her usual sparkle. Her bothersome right ankle was heavily taped and seemed to affect her tumbling.

She was nearly flawless on the unevens, making her flight from one bar to the other seem effortless. She ended the evening with a balance beam routine performed to *"Georgia."* She fell on her three consecutive layouts, but since it was an exhibition she decided to try them again. Showing a no-guts-no-glory attitude, she coolly walked back to her starting point and executed the skill perfectly.

After the exhibition, Dominique had a couple of weeks to train for a meet dubbed the "Visa Challenge: USA versus Belarus and China." She set her sights on winning.

Being a goal-oriented person helped her to accomplish her dreams by knowing where to aim. She set short-term goals in the gym for each day, like nailing eight beam routines in a row. She also had long-term goals, such as winning the all-around in Atlanta.

"I am ambitious," she declared, "and I want to work hard and go to the Olympics and win the gold—my ultimate, *ultimate*, hard-working goal. That's what I'm striving for right now."

She even listed her aspirations on a bulletin board in her bedroom. "My goal for this competition, which is the Visa Challenge, is to win the meet," she wrote. As a reminder, underneath she scrawled "100% every day effort" in big black letters.

Dominique enjoyed spending time in her room, a private

sanctuary decorated in a way that reflected her playful but determined attitude. The bedroom door sported a sign warning intruders "Danger, keep out! This room is guarded by a trained attack gymnast." On one side of the light-colored room a poster of Brad Pitt—her favorite movie star—hung on the flowered wallpaper beside an inspirational poem called "Don't Quit." On the other side, a desk beneath a window held her computer. To the left of the desk were shelves holding rows of small stuffed teddy bears. Crosses and other religious symbols looked down protectively from above her twin-sized bed while huge bear slippers peeked out from underneath a white comforter adorned with ribbons and flowers. Next to the bed was a television with more stuffed animals on top including Izzy, the mascot of the 1996 Olympic Games.

Her medals, trophies, and plaques were arranged on a bookshelf and on the walls along with framed pictures of herself from features in *International Gymnast*, *USA Gymnastics*, and *Sports Illustrated* magazines. But her most treasured awards and photographs were displayed on a built-in bookshelf next to the fireplace in the family room.

In late April, Dominique and Svetlana left for Fairfax, Virginia, the site of the Visa Challenge. Although she would have liked to compete for the United States, Svetlana was representing Belarus because there was no way for her to obtain U.S. citizenship in time for the competition or the Olympics.

Dominique's family also made the trip. "They came and surprised me," Dominique explained. "I was like, 'Wait a second, who is this?' "

In addition to her family, she ran into Toni Rand—formerly one of the owners of LaFleur's—who had an athlete, Kellee Davis, competing in the meet. Dominique and Toni enjoyed catching up with each other.

"She's very friendly," Toni said of Dominique. "She likes to talk *a lot*."

The two were chatting away when Dominique realized how much time had passed and exclaimed, "Oh! Marta's going to get mad at me; I'm talking to you. I know I shouldn't be talking right now."

Most of Dominique's contact with her old club was through her coaches. She and her former teammates had kept in contact through phone calls and letters, but as time had passed the conversations had become less frequent. Besides, none of her LaFleur's teammates were doing gymnastics anymore, although they enjoyed following Dominique's career by watching the meets on television.

At first it was difficult for her old coaches to see her with Bela, but eventually the situation improved. "I talk to them occasionally," Jeff LaFleur said about the Moceanus. "When we go to meets, I've sat with Dimitry and Camelia. We hug and we talk. I congratulate them on how well their daughter's doing, and we get along great."

The hardest thing for Dominique's former coaches to accept was how the press seemed to skip over the years she had spent training with them before going to Bela's gym. "I think it's a little disappointing when articles or TV commentaries come out and they say that she was born in California and all of a sudden she was an elite at Karolyi's and there was nothing in between," Jeff confessed. "It would just be nice to get a mention of how she got a nice start with Jeff and Julie and Beth over at LaFleur's in Tampa, then after she made the elite program she moved to Karolyi's. I don't have any bad feelings about her moving, and I knew she was going to. It's just that we worked really hard with her, and a slight mention would be encouraging. Maybe we'll develop another Dominique someday for the country."

With a tinge of hurt in her voice, Beth Hair stated, "Bela has never, ever said anything to us to acknowledge who we are. We're not expecting hardly anything—a 'thank you for this kid, you did a great job with her' or something—but no one's ever said *anything*. A lot of the stuff she's doing now were things we had her doing when she was nine. Of course, it's a lot better now because she's had all these years to work on it."

Toni explained, "Because she's been with Bela for so many years . . . it's kind of natural that this praise would be going to Bela. But certainly Jeff did an excellent job with her and developed her to the point where she was able to learn very quickly and made sure that she didn't have bad technique that would have screwed her up as she got older, which is so important. And what happens a lot of times if they get bad habits, if they're taught things poorly—bad progressions, bad basics—then you have to step back and reteach them, and I don't think Bela had to deal with that. I think he got a kid that was pretty well trained in the basic area and was able to proceed with this athlete. I think in that sense Jeff hasn't gotten enough credit."

When the press asked the Moceanus how long Dominique had been at Karolyi's, they often responded, "Since 1990." Some coaches at LaFleur's felt like Bela or someone in the Karolyi camp was telling them what to say to the media regarding specific questions so her past would be dissolved. Bela's disregard for her old coaches was still a hurtful and touchy subject years after her departure.

Jeff was baffled by what he described as a " 'this is my gymnast and no one else has ever coached her' type of attitude" from Bela. "I don't know where that comes from," he said. "It's too bad."

Announcers and commentators for gymnastics events rarely

mentioned the clubs at which a gymnast had trained before becoming well known. For example, Mary Lou Retton had only spent the last eighteen months of her career at Bela's gym before the 1984 Olympics, yet her longtime coach Gary Rafaloski was rarely mentioned or given credit for her development. This practice sometimes created a misperception among the public that a gymnast's development had taken place at only one gym. In reality, only a few top American gymnasts in recent history—like Kim Zmeskal and Dominique Dawes—had spent their entire careers at only one club. Many of them were like nomads, roaming from gym to gym trying to find the coaching situation that worked best for them.

The Visa Challenge took place over two days: vault and bars were Thursday and beam and floor were Friday. Just before the first event, Bela gave some final instructions to Dominique and Svetlana while they fastened their grips. Although Svetlana was representing Belarus, she did not sit with her Belorussian team-mates. She stayed close to Bela and Dominique.

Being coached by an American at a competition was very different for Svetlana. In the old days, her Soviet coaches had lectured her and her teammates in a tiny room before the meet, particularly if they were competing against the Americans. The Soviets had loved beating the Americans in anything they could. Svetlana had been told how bad American life was, with its drugs and violence, and that she *must* win in competitions for the government's sake. She had to be perfect. The added pressure of this win-at-any-cost attitude had once caused Svetlana to lose her love of the sport. Fortunately, coming to America had rejuvenated her interest.

In the three-minute touch warmup, Dominique went through her whole bar routine effortlessly. Bela ran from bar to bar spotting and closely watching every move. The touch warmup gave the athletes one last chance to make sure the equipment was set properly and their skills were ready. Most gymnasts did only parts of their routines in the warmup, but Bela's athletes did their whole sets. They were in top shape. Besides, the meet was usually a lot easier than practice, where they had to do their routines six to eight times.

Dominique's bar set was excellent. Her three high-flying release moves sparked the attention of the crowd, who cheered loudly upon her finish. But the audience gasped during the warmup for her second event when her hands missed the vault and she landed on her seat. A bit shaken but determined to do the vault right when it counted, she quickly stood and looked to Bela for some pointers.

When given the go-ahead, she ran hard down the runway, hit the vault—this time in the right spot—and propelled herself through the air. She brought the one-and-a-half-twisting back flip in for a solid landing and smiled. The judges, however, were not sure how to score the vault since an incorrect vault number had been displayed. Each vault that a gymnast could perform was identified by its own unique number, and the previous gymnast's number had been left on the board during Dominique's first vault.

Kelli Hill, Dominique Dawes's coach, ran over to Bela and told him about the problem. Bela had failed to notify the score flasher what vault number to post—an error that cost Dominique three-tenths. He rushed over to the head judge's table, protesting angrily and waving his arms emphatically. But Audrey Schweyer, the meet's technical director and an official familiar with Bela's outbursts, could not be swayed from her decision. Bela stormed away, and Dominique ended up with a score of 9.45.

Unaffected by the disruption, Dominique performed her second vault splendidly. Her score of 9.75 was averaged with the first for a combined 9.60, which put her in third place after the first day of competition behind Dominique Dawes and Svetlana. If not for the penalty, Dominique would have been in first.

Bela was still fuming from the controversy after the meet. "I don't know what business it was of hers," he said of Audrey Schweyer. "I think it's sickening."

Dominique looked great the next day; she did not miss a beat. On beam she flawlessly hit three layouts, a sheep jump, a front flip, and the Miller—a move named after Shannon Miller consisting of a back dive with a quarter twist to handstand followed by a half pirouette. She stuck her double back dismount cold and sauntered over to Bela, who welcomed her with open arms. She scored a 9.575, which seemed low to the fans, but the score was later corrected and upped to a 9.675.

While Dominique was tearing up the beam, things began to unravel for Svetlana and the other Dominique on floor. Svetlana fell on her Arabian double front, and Dominique Dawes opted not to compete because of a foot injury. As was the custom in such situations, she merely saluted the judges, stepped onto the floor, then saluted again and walked off.

The all-around title was now within Dominique's reach. She just had to hit her floor routine. Fortunately, her personality shined on that event. She danced, smiled, and played to the crowd between her complex tumbling sequences. Her second pass, a front handspring front full twist to a front layout and a jump, was unique. Some wondered if she meant to bounce in the air after the front layout, but Dominique insisted she did it on purpose to add a unique flare to her tumbling.

"I picked that move up from Svetlana," she said. "I noticed that when Svetlana practiced different passes on her floor routine, she did that little hop move at the end. She did this only in the gym, not in competitions. After a while I added it to my performance, just to give it a different look."[2]

For her thrilling floor set, Dominique received a 9.775—the highest score of the day—to clinch her first all-around title in the senior division. The United States won the team competition, finishing ahead of both Belarus and China.

Dominique was pleased with her victory and admitted that competing in the senior bracket was more exciting than competing with the juniors. "I had so much fun," she told television announcer Kathy Johnson after the meet. "It was great. The audience was great and I enjoyed myself competing. I haven't competed [recently because of] my injuries, but it was fun. I loved it. It was helpful, too, for my next competition."

"The Visa Challenge was a great experience for her," Dimitry said. "It was her first international event as a senior. There were no pressures because she just did what she always does at practice. She was very confident and well prepared."[3]

After the meet, Dominique was featured on the cover of *USA Gymnastics* magazine and voted the U.S. Olympic Committee's (USOC) SportsWoman of the Month for April. Television networks like ABC and NBC even came to her house and the gym for interviews.

With all of the media attention, some wondered if her schoolmates treated her like a celebrity. "Most of them don't really care," she laughed. "They don't really think of me as anyone [special]. They just call me 'short.' "

Dominique's coaches helped her learn how to be more comfortable around the press. "When you're first coming out into the spotlight, [Bela] explains it to you," Hilary Grivich said. "It's a shock at first. You don't expect all these people to have all this interest in you. He explains the types of questions they're going to be asking and the types of answers. He doesn't tell you what to say, he just gives you advice on how to get your point across."

While Bela accompanied Dominique to the major meets, Alexander and Marta did most of the coaching at home in Houston. Bela merely supervised. However, he was the main coach at his summer camps, where he was promoting Dominique as one of the attractions. His print advertisements offered campers the opportunity to "work out daily at the beautiful Waverly Hills gymnastics complex along with your favorite gymnastics stars Kim Zmeskal, Svetlana Boginskaya, and Dominique Moceanu."

Bela had three of the hottest names in gymnastics at his gym. Dominique was glad for the chance to learn from two of the sport's legends. Kim exhibited sheer power in her gymnastics, and Dominique tried to improve her tumbling and vaulting by emulating Kim's technique. She was also impressed by Svetlana's expressive dance and sharp movements.

"I look up to her," Dominique said of Svetlana. "She's very elegant. All her movements are finished. I look at her to get myself to do the same thing."[4]

"Dominique's matured so fast next to Svetlana," Bela observed. "All of a sudden, this little thing, her head is up. She's smiling. It's very promising."[5]

Svetlana was also motivated by Dominique. "When I feel tired," she explained, "I look at her and say, 'Oh my gosh, look at this kid. I can do it also.' She gave me some energy."[6]

In the early part of the summer, Dominique began having problems with her right heel. It hurt when she tumbled or punched off the springboard on vault. When it seemed to be getting worse, she went to see the team physician, Dr. Jack Jensen, who told her she had a bruised heel. He prescribed several exercises for her to do at home every day to strengthen it and instructed her to ice her foot after each practice.

"She's very easy to work with," he commented. "A common

denominator of elite athletes is that . . . they have a tremendous tenacity and they *really* get focused. So if they need to train a little harder or they're injured, they do the rehab really hard. It's a whole different level of commitment and focus."

But the injury was not the only thing bothering Dominique. She felt tired all the time as if she were not getting enough rest. Since gymnastics was on her mind most of the day, she began dreaming about competitions at night. In her dreams she sometimes did a great job, but other times she messed up her sets.

"As it turns out, while I was dreaming, my body was actually trying to perform some of the moves in my sleep," Dominique discovered. "When I woke up in the morning, I felt as if I had just run a marathon. It became impossible to do my best work in the gym, because I was exhausted and drained from exerting so much energy while I was supposed to be resting. Something had to be done."[7]

To give her body and mind a break, Dominique had to change her training program. She replaced weekend workouts with activities that kept her mind off gymnastics, like walking in the park or riding her bike. The change paid off, and she started to feel more energized.

As the U.S. Championships drew nearer, Dominique's confidence grew. She was ready and anxious to prove herself. Last year she had watched her former teammate Jennie Thompson compete against Shannon Miller and Dominique Dawes at the Championships. Now it was her turn.

Chapter 6

$\mathcal{S}parkling$

Bela fired Alexander Alexandrov in July without much warning. He then stepped in to coach Dominique and Kim full time.

"Things just weren't working out," Kim said. "And besides, Bela was intending to take over training our group, so Alexander wasn't really needed as much."

Alexander was immediately hired as the head team coach of nearby rival Brown's Gymnastics of Houston. Svetlana's allegiance was with him, so she left Karolyi's and went to Brown's. Dominique and Kim now relied on each other for motivation and daily competition as they prepared for the U.S. Championships. Shortly before the meet, the two were interviewed for a *Today* show special which aired July 19—exactly one year from the

A young Dominique contemplates her meet strategy. (© Steve Lange 1997)

The LaFleur's team in 1991 (front: Dominique Moceanu; second row: April Kaufman, Becky Waters, Becky Wildgen, Jenny Pokrana; third row: Leila Pallardy; fourth row: Tara Tagliarino, Emily Spychala; top: Jennifer Kipley, Shelly Cavaliere, Reneé Barnett). (Courtesy of Jean Pallardy)

Dominique flips onto the beam in Nashville. (© Steve Lange 1997)

Dominique dances her way to the 1994 junior national title. (© Steve Lange 1997)

Bela is right beside Dominique at her first international meet as a
senior. (© Steve Lange 1997)

Dominique displays great amplitude on her fish jump . . .

. . . and on her split leap. (© Steve Lange 1997)

Dominique shows off her *"Let's Twist Again"* floor set at the 1995 USA versus Belarus and China meet. (© Steve Lange 1997)

Dominique confidently dances through her beam routine in New
Orleans. (© Steve Lange 1997)

Bela welcomes Dominique after a scary bar dismount during the event finals at the 1995 U.S. Championships. (© Steve Lange 1997)

Moments after the mishap on bars, Dominique crashed on her beam layout, but she was solid throughout the rest of the routine. (© Steve Lange 1997)

The Karolyi's junior elites at the 1992 U.S. Classic in Tennessee.
(Courtesy of Monica Flammer)

After winning her first senior national championship, Dominique's accomplishment was posted on a sign outside the gym. (© Barry Quiner 1997)

Dominique plays to the crowd in Knoxville. (© Steve Lange 1997)

The ending pose to Dominique's debut performance of the *"Devil Went Down to Georgia"* routine. (© Steve Lange 1997)

Dominique competes on beam at the 1996 U.S. Championships with her right leg heavily wrapped. Her injury was later diagnosed as a four-centimeter stress fracture. (© Steve Lange 1997)

Though Dominique cannot compete in the 1996 Olympic Trials, Bela stretches her shoulders while the others warm up. (© Steve Lange 1997)

Dominique executes a full split on her ring leap during podium training at the 1996 Olympic Games. (© Steve Lange 1997)

Dominique hurtles toward the vault. (© Steve Lange 1997)

In a heartbreaking scene, Dominique sits down on her second and final attempt at a one-and-a-half-twisting Yurchenko vault during the team final. (© Steve Lange 1997)

The Magnificent Seven: Amanda Borden, Dominique Dawes, Amy Chow, Jaycie Phelps, Dominique Moceanu, Kerri Strug, and Shannon Miller. (© Steve Lange 1997)

Dominique dances through her floor set during the all-around final in Atlanta. (© Steve Lange 1997)

Dominique soars above the bar on her Gienger. (© Steve Lange 1997)

Dominique takes a spill on the beam which dashes her hopes for an individual medal in the event finals. (© Steve Lange 1997)

Dominique Moceanu, the youngest national champion and youngest member of the first U.S. women's gymnastics team to win an Olympic gold medal. (© Steve Lange 1997)

starting date of the 1996 Olympics. It was eye-opening for Dominique to realize the Games were only twelve months away.

Her first major test on the road to Atlanta began in August at the 1995 U.S. Championships held in New Orleans. While she was intent on winning, Bela's goals for the meet were more restrained.

"I wouldn't mind if Dominique had a strong showing in optionals and finished second," he said. "It would protect her a little from the pressure of being number one."[1] Bela knew too well how the pressure of being the favorite could destroy Dominique like it had destroyed Kim going into the 1992 Olympics. He did not intend to draw attention to his star pupil too early and subject her to additional stress. Rather, he hoped she would sneak up on everyone like Mary Lou had done in 1984.

After compulsories, Dominique was in second behind Shannon Miller. Kim had not made the trip to Louisiana because her compulsories—particularly her bar dismount—were not yet ready for competition.

On her first event in optionals, the vault, Dominique took a big hop on the landing. She looked a little nervous as Bela went over the improvements to be made, but her second attempt was solid.

"That's a good one!" Bela yelled, excitedly pumping his fist.

To everyone's surprise, Shannon toppled off the beam moments later on her three layouts.

"When I was on vault, out of the corner of my eye I saw her fall, and everybody went 'Oh!' or 'Woo,' " Dominique recalled. "I was like, 'Uh oh. I feel bad for her, but this is my chance to get ahead, maybe.' "

Bela kept the new leader warm on the sidelines by rubbing her hands and shaking her shoulders. Dominique periodically jumped up and down to keep the blood circulating. She liked being with Bela at meets because he was upbeat and motivating. He gave her the extra confidence she needed to hit her routines.

Dominique had no problems soaring above the uneven bars and dancing on the balance beam. She had a three-tenth lead over Shannon as she prepared for her final event, the floor.

"This is going to be a good event," she remembered thinking to herself. "I'm last. I can do it." Everyone else was finished competing for the night, and all eyes were on Dominique as she took her position on the floor mat. Bela rushed over to the sound system to make sure the music was cued and the volume turned up. In a last-minute appeal to the Almighty, Dimitry crossed himself with his hand before his daughter began.

Dominique exploded off the mat like a champagne cork, and she didn't stop ricocheting until she had won her first senior national title.

Bela wrapped the pint-sized phenom in his arms and exclaimed, "You won it, Domi! You won it!"

In the stands, Dominique's parents embraced in relief and joy. Bela came over and hugged the Moceanus as well.

"I was hoping and praying," Dominique said afterwards. "I wanted to [win] really bad. I did, and I'm very happy."

Everyone wanted to hear from the new champion at the press conference after the meet. "I like the attention," she told reporters, "but I'm not going to get a big head. I'll just be normal. Bela will keep me straight. I know I have to go back home and train hard. It's not going to stop me from concentrating on what I need to do. And I know what I have to do to improve."

Poised and mature, Dominique chatted comfortably with the reporters and answered their many questions. It was easy to forget she was barely a teenager, though the good-luck teddy bear peeking out of her gym bag served as a reminder.

She was only a child, to be sure, but there was no denying

that this little girl was fierce. "Some gymnasts are tigers," Bela said. "Some are little chickens. Some are rabbits. This one, she is a tiger."

Unfortunately, things did not go as smoothly for Dominique in the event finals the next day. She started well by placing third on vault. However, her hands peeled off the high bar on a double layout dismount and she hurtled through the air, flipping uncontrollably. By the grace of God she completed one flip and landed without injury, skidding to a stop on her knees. Dazed and confused, she stood and saluted the judges then walked over to Bela.

"That's a new dismount," he joked as he embraced his visibly-shaken athlete. Although he brushed the incident aside and helped Dominique prepare for her next event, Bela knew how close she had come to disaster.

"Something like that can end up a lot worse than just a surprise," he later admitted. "You slide on your knees, look around, and say, 'Thank God I'm in one piece.' "

Her family had watched the terrifying incident from the stands, and they hoped she was all right. As Dominique put the scary fall out of her mind and prepared for the balance beam, little Christina crossed her fingers hoping to bring her big sister good luck. Christina looked up to Dominique and liked to follow her around. Sometimes Christina's constant presence drove Dominique nuts and made her wish her sister would leave her alone, but other times the two were inseparable. When Christina told Dominique what a great sister she was, Dominique felt bad for ever being mean to her.

Following in Dominique's footsteps, Christina had started gymnastics classes at Karolyi's. By the age of five, she had attained level 4 and was training five days a week after school. It was difficult growing up as Dominique's little sister since the older sibling cast such a large shadow in the sport, but Dimitry and Camelia were supportive of both daughters as they strove to be their best.

"Remember, don't rush," Bela reminded Dominique before her next routine. He wanted to keep her mind busy so she would not dwell on the uneven bars fall. But the problems continued on beam. Her back foot almost missed the beam on her second layout, so her head just barely cleared it on the third. As a result, she underrotated and fell on the beam, clutching the wooden apparatus desperately in a struggle to stay on. Although she never hit the floor, the mistake still counted as a fall. Such a mishap would have rattled most gymnasts, but Dominique bravely continued her set after regaining her composure and finished without any other major errors.

"The lift wasn't there, but things are happening," Bela encouraged. "Stronger next time."

On her last event, Dominique was finally able to pull herself together. She came roaring back with an excellent floor routine that was good enough to capture the silver.

At the press conference afterwards, Bela did not want to make excuses, but he did mention that Dominique had been a little tired during the event finals. She admitted she was not used to having three continuous days of tough competition.

"I guess I was just off in my timing," she said quietly. "I was just not focused enough. I was just excited from last night, and I guess I should have been more focused on my events."

All the athletes were invited to attend a Ceremony of Honors banquet held Saturday evening after the event finals. It was a fun time for Dominique and her family. Along with Shannon and Dominique Dawes, she was voted Women's Athlete of the Year by the other national team members and coaches.

Dominique spotted her old coaches from LaFleur's after

receiving her award. "We were sitting in front of Bela," Julie LaFleur remembered. "Dominique had just gotten an award. Bela was behind us with Paul Ziert. Dominique was walking by and she happened to see us. We obviously saw her and were like, 'Dominique!' She came over and gave all of us each these great big hugs [and said], 'I miss you guys so much.' Then she pulled back into the main isle and she started walking. Bela, in his big gruff voice, said, 'Hey, what about me? You come back here and you give me a hug, too.' I don't think she saw him. She was very nervous."

Since Bela had once told her not to talk to her old coaches, she was not sure if he was angry about her affectionate display. Luckily, he merely wanted her to acknowledge him as well.

Dominique's popularity skyrocketed after the meet. She was deluged with over 6,000 pieces of fan mail and appeared on the cover of *USA Gymnastics* and *International Gymnast* magazines. Articles about America's new darling appeared in many top newspapers. She was also voted the United States Olympic Committee's SportsWoman of the Month for September. In addition, her floor music became the number-one seller in Barry Nease's Floor Express Music catalog. Budding young gymnasts everywhere wanted to be just like her and dance to the same tune.

Being so popular was quite an adjustment for Dominique. Suddenly, many people were requesting interviews, which she handled well since she was talkative and outgoing. It took some getting used to hearing from strangers that they loved her or that they collected pictures of her. Most of her fans were gymnasts who were inspired by her performances, and she felt honored by all of their nice letters. She tried to respond to as many of them as she could, but sometimes she got behind. Between practice and school, she did not have much free time.

Dominique had planned to begin the ninth grade at Northland Christian before going to the World Team Trials in Austin, Texas, but her success at Nationals changed all that. "She intended to start," school counselor Deanna Graves explained, "but I think they discovered that she was doing so well that if she was really going to go on and be successful at the Olympics, school would not be a feasible part of her life this year."

Dominique decided her school load would be too much to handle given the need for increasingly difficult practice sessions in preparation for the Games, so she opted for correspondence classes which would allow her to work at her own pace. With the help of videotaped home school lessons, she squeezed in a few hours of study between workouts.

One good thing about schooling by videotape was that she could rewind and review any sections she did not fully understand the first time. But it was difficult to get motivated about studying after a long day in the gym. Also, she did not have much of a social life. She saw few people other than family, coaches, and teammates each day. She missed her friends from school, so she dropped by occasionally to visit her old classmates and teachers. She hoped to re-enroll in regular school after the Olympics.

Dominique tried to remain focused amidst the growing pressure of the World Team Trials. Now *she* was the one to beat, with Shannon Miller, Kerri Strug, and Dominique Dawes looking to catch her. It was strange how one major victory could change things. The judges knew her, as did all the other coaches, athletes, and fans. She was the most popular gymnast in the arena and planned to use the home field to her advantage.

Dominique had suffered a pulled hamstring days before the meet, but she was determined not to let it hinder her performance at the Trials. "I kept moving it," she said. "I warmed it up pretty good. Bela helped rub it a little bit and so it was fine."

Despite a minor problem on bars that resulted in a 9.687, Dominique emerged with a slim lead over Shannon after the compulsories. She began the optionals with a tremendous bar routine followed by two near-perfect vaults. One judge even gave her a 10. She had a slight wobble on beam, but after three events she was behind Shannon by a mere thousandth of a point.

"I saw [the scoreboard] after I finished floor," Dominique later recalled. "But I didn't know right when I was going into it. I was ready for floor. I was excited to do it and I went out and did it."

Dominique scored a 9.95 on floor to squeak past Shannon, who scored a 9.912 on her last event, the beam. While Dominique was declared the winner, Shannon had actually scored more points at the Trials. In both the U.S. Championships and the World Championship Team Trials, the scores were tallied using 60% of the compulsory score and 40% of the optional score. Then 70% of the Trials' score was combined with 30% of the U.S. Championships' score. After factoring in both meets and the weightings, Dominique had come out on top.

The outcome was eerily similar to the 1992 Olympic Trials fiasco, except then Bela's gymnast had been on the losing side. Three years ago, Kim had lost to Shannon because of the same tortured team selection procedure. Bela had thrown a fit and eventually blamed Kim's downfall in part on the selection process.

This time Bela was pleased with the outcome. "I'm very glad about the way she's competing," he said. "Tonight she showed her personality, which is a fighter. That was very, very different than I ever experienced before with her. She's really turned into a tremendously aggressive athlete, and she showed it on the last event. That was more than I expected. I'm very happy."

Dominique returned home for two weeks to polish up her routines before Worlds. She was hoping to add another release move on bars and more-difficult tumbling on floor to halt recent criticism that her tumbling was not complex enough. In late September she left with Bela and Marta for Sabae, Japan, the site of the 1995 World Championships. Dominique was awestruck by the magnitude of the meet.

"I have all these feelings inside," she said. "I'm excited more than anything because this is a big meet and I want to see what's out there, to see the other competitors. This is one of the *biggest* events of my life."

Once overseas, the gymnasts had a week to adjust to the time zone change and gel as a team. Dominique Dawes and Amy Chow had been unable to travel at the last minute, so two relatively unknown gymnasts—Theresa Kulikowski and Mary Beth Arnold—had taken their places. Amanda Borden and Jennie Thompson were also out with injuries, which hurt the depth of the team. It would not be easy for the fragmented group, but with Shannon Miller, Kerri Strug, Jaycie Phelps, and Doni Thompson rounding out the squad, the U.S. was hoping to defend its silver medal from the 1994 World Team Championships.

In the team compulsories, Dominique had a problem on her first event that led to a small controversy. She did not complete her cast to handstand during her bar routine, which prevented her from going on to the next move, a half pirouette, so she swung down and tried the skill again. She finished her set without any other mistakes and was given a 9.437. Some thought the score was a bit high since she had repeated several elements. However, the judges claimed that Dominique had only taken an extra swing, which incurred a mere three-tenth penalty.

Dominique was solid on her remaining three events to finish seventh. Despite problems on beam, the Americans were in second place behind Romania after compulsories. But it was going to be tough for the inexperienced group to hold onto their high standing in optionals. It only made matters worse when Shannon sprained her ankle on a beam dismount during a training session. The picture looked bleak for the Americans.

The U.S. began optionals on bars. As was the custom, the team with the highest score after compulsories began on vault, the team with the second highest score began on bars, the third place team began on beam, and the fourth place team began on floor. The higher a team placed, the better its order of events in the optionals.

The Americans looked strong on bars. Dominique had a slight problem with her new release move, a Pak salto, but she covered nicely. She roared back with a superb routine on beam, which was quickly becoming her best event. Unfortunately, as in the compulsories, the U.S. had two low scores on beam, although it helped that each team was allowed to drop its lowest score on each event.

Dominique was outstanding on floor, but low scores from newcomers Theresa and Mary Beth dropped the team to third behind China. The Americans hoped to improve their position on the final event, but the first several scores were average—not great. It looked as though the U.S. might slip into fourth behind Russia.

Dominique was up last. On her first attempt, her right hand almost missed the vault, so she was able to complete only one of her intended one-and-a-half twists. She needed at least a 9.60 to beat the Russians, but with the error her score for the first vault was far from adequate. She slowly walked back to her starting marker feeling the weight of the team on her shoulders.

Dominique had one more try. With determination blazing in her eyes, she ran down the runway and hammered the springboard. Both hands found the vault this time, and she pushed off, flipping once and twirling one-and-a-half times. She took a small step on the landing, but the vault was solid. She scored a 9.612 to clinch the bronze for the Americans.

In a rare show of esprit de corps, the team gathered for a group hug. "You guys pulled together and everybody did their job," exulted assistant coach Mary Lee Tracy. "That was awesome. You did the best we could do today."

Bela chimed in, "Let me tell you honestly: congratulations to everybody. Good job, guys."

While the U.S. managed to win the team bronze, observers gave them very low marks for team unity in Sabae. *International Gymnast* publisher Paul Ziert wrote in an editorial, "Thumbs down [to] the U.S. women's team for showing absolutely no sign of working together as a team. In fact, one journalist proclaimed that 'it's good that the American girls have USA on their uniform or we would never guess that they're competing on the same team.' "

Each athlete had been almost entirely focused on herself. While gymnastics was an individual sport and the gymnasts were not accustomed to paying attention to what others were doing, the U.S. women had seemed hard-pressed to even acknowledge one another. Some attributed this lack of camaraderie to the coaches, who—with the exception of Mary Lee—kept the athletes segregated. Left to themselves, they probably would have encouraged and cheered for each other.

"Dominique pretty much stays to herself in training, as I am sure that is the way Bela wants it," national coach John Geddert noted. "She does not cheer for the others on the team, but I am not sure if this is on purpose or not. It may be that she is focusing on her own job at hand."

When asked what the team had done together outside the

gym, Kerri responded, "Nothing. We didn't do anything. Well, we did one thing, but Dominique didn't come with us. We got to put on kimonos. They dressed us up and took pictures, but other than that we didn't do anything."

The U.S. team spent most of the trip at the gym or in the hotel, with no time for sightseeing or shopping. Dominique even spent her fourteenth birthday in Japan but did not celebrate properly until she got home.

"We all signed a card, and I think she got a little stuffed animal," Kerri remembered. "It was right before the competition, so they didn't want to do anything to mess up our training."

After finishing eighth overall in the team competition, Dominique looked forward to the all-around where she hoped to win a medal. Bela, however, still had reservations about her winning too much too soon.

"I don't want her to be great too early and have that pressure like Kim did," he said, referring to Kim's 1991 World Championship victory shortly before the 1992 Olympics. He knew what the pressure of being the top-ranked gymnast could do in an Olympic competition. He also knew how the press would hound the favorite. "I want her to just have a solid competition so we can build up. Slow, steady preparation. That's our strategy for '96."[2]

Dominique was nervous as she warmed up for the all-around competition. This would be the biggest meet of her career next to the Olympics. The competitive field was tough and experienced, and this was her first match against many of them. She recognized several of the foreign gymnasts from magazines and televised meets.

Generally, in the year before the Olympics, all the athletes hoping to compete in the Games competed at Worlds. The Romanians had sent their best, Lavinia Milosovici and Gina Gogean. The top Russians, Svetlana Khorkina and Dina Kochetkova, were also present. China had its star—Mo Huilan—while the Ukraine had ace athlete Lilia Podkopayeva. The Belorussian powerhouses Svetlana Boginskaya and Elena Piskun were ready to fight. And everyone was out to dethrone the reigning two-time World Champion, Shannon Miller.

In addition to all the new faces, members of the news media were everywhere. Dominique had to get used to ever-present cameramen and an incessant barrage of questions from reporters. Even the *Daily Yomiuri*, the local newspaper, was touting Dominique as a future celebrity in the sport.

Thankfully, only the athletes and coaches were allowed in the practice gym. There Dominique could concentrate on her routines and block out distractions.

"I try not to think about the pressure," she said. "I'm just going to try to do my best, and just go out there and go strong and do the best that I can because I know I can do it."

Dominique began on the balance beam, and she was the first gymnast up. Being placed early in the lineup was usually disadvantageous since judges tended to give lower scores to the first few gymnasts. The rationale for this was they needed to leave room to give higher scores to later competitors in case their routines were better.

Dominique was a bit hesitant throughout the routine, suffering slight breaks on her three layouts and her front flip. She did not complete the Miller move, opting for only a back handspring with a quarter twist. However, she solidly stuck her dismount. She knew there had been problems with the routine but was relieved to have this difficult event behind her. Being first on the most nerve-wracking apparatus in her World all-around debut had been a challenge, and she had passed the test—maybe not with the highest marks, but at least she had not succumbed to the pressure by falling. If she had the misfortune of starting on beam in Atlanta, this experience would help her be more prepared.

On her next event, Dominique charmed the crowd with her playful and expressive dance. She smiled, hopped, and wiggled her way into their hearts. Her only mistake was a step out of bounds on her second tumbling pass.

Dominique was outstanding on vault, sticking her first attempt cold. Her uneven bar set was equally magnificent. She seemed to improve with each routine, getting more and more comfortable as the meet progressed. She was realizing that she had to be confident and aggressive if she wanted to be competitive on the world's stage.

Dominique wound up fifth in the all-around. Since Tatiana Gutsu had finished fifth at the 1991 World Championships then had gone on to win the 1992 Olympics, Dominique hoped it was a good omen.

Bela was pleased with Dominique's placement. He knew less pressure meant more of an advantage in the long run.

"She was surrounded by former World Champions, and she was high enough to be visible but not high enough to be a target," he explained after the meet. "It's exactly how I would like it to be."[3]

Dominique, on the other hand, was not completely satisfied. "I thought at the end I could hold onto third place, but it didn't happen," she said at the press conference after the meet. "Maybe next time."

The last competition of the World Championships was the event finals in which the top eight finishers on each event after the team competition—limited to only two per country—challenged for the gold on each apparatus. Dominique had qualified to two event finals: beam and floor exercise. At the last minute, she was also given the opportunity to compete on vault. Kerri had injured her right ankle during the warmup and was unable to compete, leaving Dominique, the alternate, to fill her spot. But Dominique had not had enough time to warm up, so she decided not to vault.

On balance beam she was exquisite, executing every move with confidence and class. She scored a 9.837 to tie for the lead with Lilia, the new World Champion. It looked as though Dominique might win the gold until Mo outdid everyone with a spectacular routine that earned a 9.90 and first place. Dominique graciously accepted the silver, the first and only individual medal won by the Americans, as her parents, who had also made the trip to the Far East, beamed proudly from the stands.

Dominique began her floor exercise with a strong full-twisting double pike somersault. Unfortunately, her left wrist brace came un-Velcroed after her first tumbling pass. As she danced and tumbled through the routine, the pesky strap unraveled and dangled in the air. Besides distracting the audience and judges, it seemed to throw Dominique off mentally. She over-rotated her last tumbling pass, landing her two-and-a-half twist punch front flip out of bounds and putting her hand on the floor. The routine ended and she trudged over to Bela, biting her lip in anticipation of his less-than-thrilled reception. The fall and the step out of bounds were costly; she placed seventh with a 9.087.

The wrist-brace fiasco had been yet another in a series of freak incidents that had beset Dominique in event finals during the past two months. First there had been her dangerous flight on bars at the U.S. Championships, then the fall on beam, and now this at Worlds. She hoped to get the mishaps out of the way before the Olympics.

After the event finals, the media was anxious to talk with the new superstar from the United States. When asked about her impressions of the meet, Dominique said, "It felt great, and I was happy to be the only American up there on the medal podium.

The experience here makes me excited for Atlanta."

One reporter asked her to grade herself. "B-plus," she concluded. But upon further reflection, she reconsidered: "An A, maybe?"

Marta, who was nearby, shook her head and smiled. "Her confidence is coming on."

A farewell party was held for all the athletes after the event finals. Dominique was stunning in a dress of black velvet and hunter green. A long cameo necklace and a gold arm bracelet completed the ensemble. She mingled with members of the Romanian team and met several of her international rivals.

Bela decided it was time for Dominique to change her floor routine. She had been using the same music for over a year, and Bela thought she needed an updated routine for the Olympics.

Geza Pozsar and Dominique got to work. "We tried to make up a modern Russian-type thing, and she didn't like it," Geza said. "We tried to make a change from the rock-and-roll style to more dramatic, but it wasn't her. It was an okay routine—it wasn't bad—but her personality did not come out so sharply, and she wasn't excited about it."

They tried to change the music a little and redo some of the dance elements, but nothing seemed to work. Finally, Dominique told Bela she wanted something different, so it was back to the drawing board for new music. She never competed the dramatic routine.

Based upon her performance at Worlds, Dominique was invited to the Atlanta Gymnastics Invitational held November 16-17 in the venue to be used for the Olympic Games. Unfortunately, she had to decline the invitation because of a kidney infection. But three weeks later she was healthy and able to participate in a fun professional meet, the Rock 'n Roll Gymnastics Championships held December 7 in Charleston, South Carolina.

The format of this meet was unique. Each athlete had to perform two floor routines before a panel of celebrity judges: Miss South Carolina Danielle Corley, volleyball great Karch Kiraly, Olympic swimmer Pablo Morales, famous recording artist Eddie Rabbit, and Czechoslovakian figure skater Josef Sabovcik. The night before the meet, a figure-skating competition with a similar format took place at which Dominique met such stars as Scott Hamilton and Kristi Yamaguchi.

Decked out in a dark blue leotard with white lace, Dominique performed her first floor routine to the tune *"Chantilly Lace."* Following the entertaining set, she joined Bela on the performers' couch to await her scores. She received four 10s and one 9.90.

Dominique was having a good time. "It was fun out there," she told former gymnast and ESPN commentator Kurt Thomas. "It was great!" She and Geza had enjoyed putting the special routine together.

On her second routine she needed perfect 10s to outdo Kim Zmeskal. She did just that. Her performance to *"Baby Likes to Rock It"* enthralled the audience and—more importantly—the five judges, who each gave her a 10.

"This crowd is wonderful!" she exclaimed after her routine. "They're awesome! Everybody's getting into it, and that's great for the floor." She hopped up on the couch and waved to both sides of the arena, eliciting even louder screams from the fans.

Dominique won first place, and the prize was an electric guitar. "I think it's wonderful," she said of her award. "When I saw it last night with the ice skaters winning it, I was like, 'Wow, I want to get that.' So I just went out there and had fun."

Bela was equally pleased. "Tonight, I believe she's a winner," he said. "Not just because she got the beautiful guitar but because she got the feeling of playing to the crowd."

When Dominique arrived home, she put her prize on display in her bedroom. Whenever she glanced at it, it reminded her of how much fun the meet had been.

As the Christmas season arrived, Dominique looked forward to the festivities. She enjoyed a team party where everyone performed skits and exchanged gifts. Then the group spent the night at the gym. The next morning, Christmas Eve, they had an abbreviated workout. Although it was not much of a break, Bela gave everyone Christmas day and the day after off. They could not miss more than two days because the Olympics were only seven months away, and they had a lot of work to do before then. On Christmas morning, Dominique enjoyed opening presents with her family. She especially liked being surprised by unexpected gifts.

As the exciting and eventful year came to a close, Dominique was voted the USOC Female Gymnast of the Year. She was also nominated for the USOC SportsWoman of the Year award, where she finished seventh in the ranking. In addition, she was named a finalist for the Amateur Athletic Union's Sullivan Award.

Dominique had definitely made her mark on the gymnastics community. She was now the best gymnast in America and one of the best in the world—an enviable position with the Olympics just around the corner.

Chapter 7

Noticed

The start of the new year brought some immediate changes to Dominique's life. For one, her dad left his job at the car dealership to open his own used-car lot. In addition, the Moceanus decided to add a bathroom to the back of the house and expand Dominique's bedroom. An admitted pack rat, she liked to keep *everything*, and her countless awards and stuffed animals had filled her room to overflowing.

In the gym, Dominique welcomed some familiar faces back to the team: Kerri Strug and Svetlana Boginskaya.

Explaining why she had left in the first place, Kerri said, "I knew I was getting older and my parents and I were kind of afraid that if I kept training real intensely with Bela, I wouldn't be able to handle it—not just physically, but mentally." She had gone searching for a more relaxed atmosphere and had tested several top gyms in the country, like Brown's, Dynamo, and the Colorado Aerials. But the lighter regimen at these gyms had left her feeling less prepared for competitions. With the Olympics drawing nearer, she had realized she needed more intense training. And for her, that could only come from one gym.

"Since I left Bela's, I've always had expectations of what training should be like," she remarked. "But nobody trains like he does . . . not even Steve Nunno. It's been hard to adapt to anyone else's style. Even though it's really hard, Karolyi's is the best."[1]

Svetlana returned a few weeks after Kerri. It was surprising that she would leave former Soviet coach Alexander Alexandrov in favor of Bela, but she felt that training with him was the best way to reach her goal of competing in a third Olympics. Besides, she admitted that she longed for those early-morning workouts and late-night practice sessions.

In the past four years, Dominique had been one of the few gymnasts vying for the 1996 Olympic team who had remained at one gym. Of the people with whom she had trained, Jennie had switched back and forth between Karolyi's and Dynamo several times, Kerri had been to five different clubs in the four years since the 1992 Olympics, and Svetlana had switched from Karolyi's to Brown's and back.

It was risky to disrupt training and try other programs. Indeed, club hopping had cost Dianne Durham and Kristie Phillips their chances at making the Olympic team. It took time to adjust to new coaches, a new atmosphere, and a new style of training. In addition, when an athlete changed gyms, her new coaches often wanted to redo all of her existing routines. Dominique benefitted from consistent training with instructors who knew her strengths and weaknesses. She was comfortable with her coaches and her daily routine.

While Kerri and Svetlana had returned to Karolyi's, Kim had decided to discontinue her comeback attempt. "My knee is perfectly all right, so I don't think right now my knee is to blame," she said, referring to the knee injury that had sidelined her in 1994. "What kind of made me come to this decision is that I had to wait so long in the rehab that things started eating away at me—seeing Dominique go to all these competitions in that year-and-a-half while I was sitting back at home trying to get everything back. . . . A lot of it had to do with the time that I had to wait. I wasn't able to spend the summer training in '94 like I had planned and then start competing again immediately."

Kim also noted that her feelings about gymnastics had changed. "The fun part of it and the joy that I had for the sport was starting to go away, so that's why I decided to kind of step back," she said. She began enjoying a new life that included having a boyfriend and starting college. In the future, she planned to stay involved with professional meets and the post-Olympic tour. "I will never look back on it as a bad experience. I'm glad I did that because of the people that were associated with my working out again. I think the most important thing in my life is the people around me."

While Kim's career was winding down, Dominique was gearing up for the toughest year of her life. Her first appearance of the Olympic year was at the January 14 Reno Team Challenge. Bart and Nadia served as team captains for this unique battle of the sexes that included four events: vault, still rings versus balance beam, high bar versus uneven bars, and floor. On each event, four male gymnasts went head-to-head against four female gymnasts in individual winner-take-all duels each worth ten points. In addition, ten bonus points—determined by audience applause—were awarded after each round. The team with the highest total at the end won.

The first event for both the men and the women was vault. Dominique was the last one up for her team. She was pitted against Mark Booth, who did an excellent one-and-a-half-twisting Yurchenko. Dominique knew she would have to do very well to beat him, so she opted for a vault she thought she could stick, a half-twisting Yurchenko. But she had a little too much power at the end and took a big lunge forward. Mark's score of 9.90 easily surpassed Dominique's 9.65. She was a little disappointed in her performance, but showing good sportsmanship she congratulated Mark by shaking his hand before heading back to her seat. The teams gathered on the floor exercise mat for the bonus round, and the thunderous applause for the women was just enough to give them the extra points despite the men's attempt to garner cheers by performing Thomas flairs on the floor.

Dominique was up against John Roethlisberger in the next round. John went first, executing a great rings routine complete with a stuck dismount. Dominique had her work cut out for her. She started her beam set with a unique shoulder roll invented by former Romanian gymnast Daniela Silivas, easily executed all of her daring moves, and stuck the landing. After saluting the judges, she ran over to the announcer and stood opposite John, who playfully shook his finger at her.

"Ladies and gentlemen," the announcer began. "For the men, John Roethlisberger scores 9.60." John's jaw dropped as he spread his arms in disbelief at the low score. He even turned and pretended like he was going to run over to the judges and tear into them. "And for Dominique Moceanu," the announcer continued, "9.90!"

Dominique beamed and waved to the crowd. When she extended her arm to shake John's hand, he grabbed her in mock fury and carried her across the mat.

Dominique's actual score had been a 9.95, but the announcer had read it incorrectly. Regardless, she was happy to contribute ten points to the women's total. The men did standing back flips to win the bonus round, tying the score at fifty points apiece at the halfway mark.

Dominique did not do bars, but she was the anchor for the team on floor where she had to battle Mike Racanelli. Before they began, Nadia and Dominique tried to intimidate the men by thumbing their noses at Bart and Mike. Their teasing did not seem to work, however, as Mike turned in a stellar performance. Not be outdone, Dominique nailed all of her tumbling passes and finished the routine by pointing arrogantly but playfully at Mike. The crowd erupted with delight.

The judges gave Mike a 9.70, and they awarded Dominique a 10. Upon hearing her score, she raised her clenched fists in triumph and jumped up and down with excitement.

In a desperate grab for points, the men shed their shirts and flexed for the audience in the bonus round. The women, who were not quite as creative and much more modest, merely gestured to the crowd to cheer for them. The fans preferred the men's brazen display and gave them ten points to tie the score at 110 each.

The meet ended with a tumble-off. Dominique pulled out all the stops with a back-to-back tumbling run—a maneuver that had made another Dominique famous. She did a one-and-a-half twist through to a back flip punch front, then she headed back across the mat with a roundoff, three back handsprings, and a double back.

It was up to the audience to decide the winner. This time, they overwhelmingly favored the women. Knowing the deck was stacked against them, the men bowed before the women with arms outstretched as if to say "We're not worthy." At the end of a tight race, the women were declared the winners, and a donation to the Special Olympics was made on their behalf.

In late February, Dominique traveled to Fort Worth, Texas, for the 1996 American Cup. But three days before the meet she decided not to compete because of a recurring pain in her left heel. Her doctor suspected she might be developing Sever's disease, a serious inflammation of the growth plate in her heel.

"The doctor recommended that Dominique avoid hard landings for a short time," Bela announced at a press conference. "Although we are disappointed she can't compete in the American Cup, we feel it's in her best interests. Dominique experienced the same type of pain in her right heel last year, and we avoided hard landings and it's fine now."

"I'm growing right now," Dominique said. "It's from a lot of pounding on it. It's getting better. I've been doing routines until a couple days before the meet and we had to take the mats out and start landing on the hard surfaces. Then it started to hurt too much. Bela said, 'Let's not do this. This was a good meet, but we'd rather save you, get your heel better, and be healthy before you hurt yourself even more.' So Bela and I both decided it was better if I didn't go."

John Geddert, a coach whose athlete Katie Teft also suffered heel problems, said, "If her heel injury is *truly* Sever's disease and if it is a severe case, then I would say she is in trouble. . . . It is like someone stabbing you in the back of your heel every time you punch the floor, vault board, or beam. The worst thing about it is that there is very little you can do to eliminate the pain."

While Dominique did not compete, she was still expected to practice as usual. Bela did not let her relax in workout. She had to learn how to work through the pain like her predecessors had done.

"I had several injuries and I pushed through them," Betty Okino said. "Now they're all fine. I'm completely healed. At the time they hurt terribly and I didn't think they'd ever heal and I thought I'd break in half. But it's not true at all. Your body has a way of healing itself. You know your own limits. If you absolutely can't do it, your body's going to give out on you, then you'll stop. But until that point, you're capable."

It was scary for Dominique to be suffering from a serious injury only a few months before the Olympics. "I've really been talking to her and her folks a lot because of the timing," Dr. Jack Jensen said. "There's just not time to be hurt."

Although she was not competing at the American Cup, Dominique received the McDonald's Break Through to Be Your Best Award and a $1,000 grant toward her training.

Before the meet began, Dominique returned home to Houston. She watched the competition from the gym. "I wish I was there," she pined to the commentators via satellite. "I'd love to compete and have fun out there. Seeing everyone [makes me] want to jump into the TV and go out there and perform."

Bela's other two entries, Kerri and Svetlana, went on to finish one and two, respectively. Kerri looked strong and seemed happy to be back at Karolyi's.

"A lot of things have changed, definitely for the better," she said. "I feel more comfortable being there. . . . Bela and I are working together rather than me following."[2]

Two days later on March 4, Dominique was honored at the Walt Disney World Yacht and Beach Club in Lake Buena Vista, Florida, as one of ten finalists for the Amateur Athletic Union's (AAU) Sullivan Award. Established in 1930 in honor of James E. Sullivan, the founder and former president of the AAU, this "Oscar" of sports awards was the highest honor in U.S. amateur athletics. At a black-tie banquet, each nominee was given a medal and a chance to say a few words. Dominique was not able to make it to the ceremony, but she spoke by way of videotape. "The Olympics are very close, so I will be training hard," she said from the gym, "and I won't get to be there with you guys, but I thank you all for supporting me and nominating me. I really appreciate it. I think it's a great event. I'm really excited that I was nominated. I want to thank my parents and coaches for supporting me. Hopefully, I'll be there next time."

After her speech, Bryant Gumbel, the master of ceremonies, joked, "She couldn't be here; it's past her bedtime, anyway."

Olympic speedskater Dan Jansen, who had won the award the previous year, announced the winner. Bruce Baumgartner, an Olympic wrestler, finally won after being nominated five years in a row. If Dominique had won, she would have been the youngest recipient in the history of the award.

Dominique had to avoid some major competitions in the spring because of her heel. Besides the American Cup, she did not participate in the Individual Apparatus World Championships in Puerto Rico. Still, she was thankful when her heel diagnosis was downgraded from Sever's disease to merely a bad bruise.

Bela was not too upset about his athlete missing the Individual Apparatus Worlds because he thought it was a poorly-timed meet with the U.S. Championships and the Olympic Trials looming on the horizon. "It is absolutely against the best interests of the athletes," he declared. "I would not take the chance to put unnecessary stress and unnecessary risk on their physical and mental health."[3] He remembered how Kim had won the beam and floor events at the Individual Apparatus Worlds only to be underscored a few months later in Barcelona, and he did not see how the meet could help Dominique's quest for gold in Atlanta.

While recuperating from her heel injury, Dominique participated in several exhibitions at various gymnastics clubs. She performed her normal bar routine but took out most of the difficulty on beam to protect her foot from hard landings on the wooden apparatus. She did, however, introduce a new skill on beam—Bela claimed she was the only one in the world to do it—comprised of a Miller followed by an extra half turn. It had only taken her a few months to master this complex skill. If she were the first person to compete the skill internationally, it would be named after her.

Dominique answered questions from spectators after the exhibitions, handling even the toughest in her usual polite and cheery way. Her vibrant personality and infectious grin attracted many fans.

"I don't think I could fake it because it wouldn't look right," she said about her smile. "I just go out there—I love to smile. It's all about me. I'm always having fun. I like to smile."

Although Dominique had the ideal shape and size for gymnastics, Bela believed her biggest asset was her personality. "I know she has the personality like no other athlete for a long, long time," he said. "With her personality and with her bubbly way of performing, she really, in my vision, can become a role model in gymnastics, which would be a very, very positive thing."

"I hope to be one of the Mary Lou [types]—you know, a jumpy person," Dominique claimed. "I think it's great to be somebody like that. You always attract somebody when you smile. You always catch somebody's attention."

Some believed Dominique's personality was a breath of fresh air that the sport desperately needed to counter recent media assertions that female gymnasts were merely the hapless, half-starved victims of unhealthy parental pressures and unbridled coaches' egos. Bernie Lincicome, a reporter for the *Chicago Tribune*, described these athletes as "grim little muscle balls who bounce from apparatus to apparatus with all the joy of a thief looking for an unlocked car."[4]

"I think this image, that there's only unhappy little girls training in gyms under coaches that are mean and only want what *they* want, is not true," said national coach Toni Rand. "I think that Dominique could be the one to break through that barrier and tell them that 'No, we're not all that way. We do smile. We do have lives. We are happy. We enjoy being here. We like our coaches. We like our parents. We don't throw up. We don't have to do all the stuff that they say we do just to be an athlete.' "

Certainly, Dominique's personality was having a positive impact on the sport, but some detected a hint of arrogance in her otherwise irresistible demeanor. "It is what separates her from the rest of the pack," John Geddert said. "As gymnastics talents go, she is good but by no means a Shannon Miller as far as physical talent goes. She is a picture of confidence; she walks it and she talks it. Some may say that she is on the conceited side."

Bela recognized that Dominique was full of self-confidence—"sometimes too much." He explained, "She's Ms. Confidence. . . . She loves to show off. She loves to conquer. It's like she's in seventh heaven when people applaud."[5]

In the spring, Svetlana left Karolyi's to train back home in Minsk. Some Belorussian coaches had been voicing their resentment of Bela for coaching Svetlana. Bela did not care much about their complaints. Once, he even slapped his behind to indicate where the Belorussian coaches could kiss him. But others involved with the sport wondered how Bela would be able to coach Svetlana during the Olympic team competition since she would not be with the American team.

"Many people in the American [gymnastics] federation don't like it that he has devoted so much time to me," Svetlana said, "but Bela stands his ground. But I think we've come to a parting of the ways, even though the Olympics aren't here yet. He has to give all his attention to the American national team now. That's partly why you're seeing me in Belarus."[6]

Once Svetlana departed, the criticism subsided. Bela was left to concentrate solely on his American athletes, Kerri and Dominique. In April he had Geza come out for a week to begin working on a new floor routine for Dominique. It usually took about three to five hours to come up with a new routine, then for the next several days there were little changes to be made to fix rough spots.

Geza created the routine by listening to the music to decide where the tumbling passes should go then building the dance around the tumbling. But he did not make it up all by himself; he and Dominique developed the routine together. Both played around with ideas and decided which ones worked the best. Geza wanted Dominique to like the routine because he knew her performance would suffer if she were not comfortable with it.

"She has her own little ideas," Geza remarked. "Sometimes they are very good. She's starting now to get that feeling and experience to have her own style."

While Geza was the routine's choreographer, Barry Nease had arranged the music: *"Devil Went Down to Georgia,"* picked especially for the fans in Atlanta. Bela had come up with the idea for the music when he heard the country song on the radio one day.

After Geza, Bela brought in another specialist to work with his two stars. Artur Akopyan, a member of the 1979 and 1981 gold-medal-winning World Championship Soviet team who had won individual golds on high bar at the '81 Worlds and vault at the '83 Worlds, helped Dominique improve the new skills she was hoping to add to her routines for the Olympics. She was practicing a new bar dismount—a full-twisting double layout somersault—but putting it into her routine was not easy since she was usually very tired by the end. On floor she was hoping to do either a double back layout or a double front flip. She worked on several different tumbling passes; Bela would decide which ones to use as the Olympics got closer. On beam she refined her new skill and worked on a full-twisting double back dismount.

With only three months until the Games, a terrorist scare momentarily diverted Dominique's concentration away from gymnastics and onto her own safety. Authorities learned from an informant about a small militia group located just outside Atlanta with plans to build and distribute pipe bombs. Some wondered if they intended to harm participants at the Olympics.

"Who would want to spoil an Olympic dream?" Dominique wondered. "Who would want to do something like that? People should just be happy and proud that there's an event like this in our own country. They should do whatever they can to help the Games, not hurt them."

Bela seemed unconcerned. "Let me tell you," he said, "this is probably more important for the media than us. If I were to start to worry about a wacko with plans to disturb the Olympics, that would be too bad."[7]

Understandably, the incident raised questions about athlete security and brought to mind the 1972 Olympics in Munich where eleven Israeli athletes and coaches had been killed by Palestinian terrorists. But Dominique pushed her fears to the back of her mind and continued training as usual.

Despite the threat, she went to the Olympic City for a media summit hosted by the United States Olympic Committee on April 26. Journalists from all over the country were invited to interview potential Olympians from different sports. Dominique sat casually in a plush armchair—feet dangling inches above the floor—and answered questions for about an hour. She talked about her childhood and how she had first begun gymnastics. Bela, who sat beside her in a suit, also took questions. Nadia had invited him to her wedding that same weekend, but Bela had declined so he could be with Dominique. He was not completely comfortable with all this media attention being focused on his athlete.

"No matter how much I would like to keep her out of this, there's no way," Bela told the reporters. "[Before], the media did not care about the individual celebrities until after the event was done. Today is different. People are interested in younger, outstanding individuals, and they want to showcase them before the performances. I don't think anybody can stop this trend."

Dominique's parents and coaches tried to screen her phone calls and shelter her from unnecessary publicity. However, they agreed to several commercial appearances and interviews. Dominique was featured in a thirty-second television commercial and in print ads for Visa. The credit card company was a major sponsor of the Olympic Games, and a portion of all its credit card sales went toward helping Olympic athletes. Dominique was also in a Kodak ad. During the filming she met former boxing great Muhammed Ali, Olympic sprinter Florence Griffith Joyner, and legendary Olympic decathlete Bob Mathias. She also appeared in a montage of inspiring sports images used in the music video of *"Reach"* by Gloria Estefan, the official Olympic theme song. In addition, she participated in a two-day photo shoot with photographer-to-the-stars Annie Leibovitz for her book entitled Olympic Portraits and the cover of the May issue of *Vanity Fair.*

"She's fourteen going on sixty-five," Annie joked. "An interesting thing about the young girl gymnasts is that they look like they're carrying the world on their backs."

Other national magazines such as *Cosmopolitan, Glamour,*

People, Newsweek, Sports Illustrated, Star, 'Teen, and *Time* could not resist doing features on Dominique before the Games. She was comfortable but guarded around the press, aware of how easily they might twist her words. She also knew how displeased Bela and her parents would be if she said something inappropriate.

She had not always been so sophisticated. At the age of ten, she had once spoken too freely to *Time* magazine about Bela. "He gets real mad," she had divulged. "On occasion, he kicks kids out of the gym. But the worst is when he says nothing, and you don't know what's the matter. He's much nicer [at meets]."[8]

On May 1, a few days after returning from the media summit, Bela and Marta announced they were selling their Houston gym. They intended to retire after the Olympics and live at the ranch.

"I think this is enough for us," Marta confessed. "We are not going to be there in 2000." Although they planned to continue operating their summer camps, they did not plan to be involved with the day-to-day coaching of elite athletes.

The Karolyis sold the club to former coach James Holmes, who also owned the Acrofit Gymnastics Center outside Houston. In a letter to their gymnasts and parents, the Karolyis wrote, "We are very confident that James, who was our associate for more than ten years in our program, will run the same quality program as we have been striving for. We wish everybody the best of luck and an enjoyable athletic career in the most beautiful sport in the world."

The announcement did not come as a big surprise since Bela had come out of retirement to coach athletes training for the 1996 Olympics, but it was still disappointing for all the future Karolyi protégées.

"After selling our house to move closer to the gym and give our daughter the opportunity to train in one of the best programs in the world, we can only wait and see what the future holds," observed one parent. "The Karolyis have every right to retire. Unfortunately, the coaches left behind, the stability of the program, and the future of the kids that have invested hundreds of hours and lots of money to be with the Karolyis is now uncertain."

James planned to take over the gym on June 1. He hoped to maintain a good relationship with Bela and wanted to leave the door open in case Bela changed his mind about retiring.

"The purpose and main reason for buying his gym was because we knew that Bela would maintain an association with that gym if there was a person in there he felt some obligations to," the new owner said.

It was sad to think of the big yellow-and-black sign that read "Karolyi's Gymnastics" coming down. At least for the time being, James intended to keep things as they were.

"We will maintain for a short period of time Bela's name on the gym," he said. "Obviously, this is the Olympic year and it's going to stimulate some activity—negative or positive it doesn't matter. The name is out there and it's an endorsement. . . . At least through December, we'll maintain the Karolyi's Gymnastics name."

Dominique traveled to the Colorado Springs Olympic Training Center in May for the U.S. Classic. All of the best U.S. gymnasts were there: Shannon Miller, Kerri Strug, Jennie Thompson, Amanda Borden, Dominique Dawes, and Amy Chow.

Dominique began solidly in compulsories, scoring the highest on every event. She enjoyed a lead of over six tenths going into the optional round. However, she and Bela decided it would be best if she did not compete in optionals. She had already qualified to the U.S. Championships and had only come to the Classic to compete compulsories because it was her last chance to be judged on them before Nationals. Besides, she competed optionals all the time. In addition, she did not want to risk injury or the loss of her number-one status.

Opting not to stay even to watch the optionals, she and Bela flew home Saturday morning. In Dominique's absence, Jennie stepped up and grabbed the title.

After the U.S. Classic, it was time for Dominique to pack. She was moving her training to Bela's ranch to concentrate on making the Olympic team. Besides, Bela no longer owned the Houston gym.

"I'm bringing all my leotards, all my shirts, all my stuffed animals, and my clock," she told a cheerless Christina, who looked on from her perch on Dominique's bed. She was going to miss her big sister.

"She's going to stay out there," Christina said sadly. "She's *never* going to come home."

The rules were strict at the ranch. Dominique could not talk on the phone; her only outside correspondence was through letters. In addition, she saw her family only on weekends.

While Dominique missed her parents and sister, she turned her attention to the job at hand. She had a lot of intense training ahead. With less than two months until the Games, there was no time to waste.

Chapter 8

Trials and Tribulations

Dominique's confidence was building as the Olympics approached. She heard Bela say "No, that's not right!" less and "That was a good one!" more.

"He's helped me so much and been supportive all the time," Dominique said. "Everything is working according to plan."

Bela was optimistic as well. "Everything just came at the right time and at the right moment," he observed.

Over the years, Dominique and Bela had grown closer. She felt more comfortable talking with him than she had when she first arrived four years earlier. She trusted him and believed he could make her dreams come true.

Nadia thought Dominique could strike gold in Atlanta. She believed in Bela's coaching and regarded Dominique's Romanian heritage as an advantage.

"She has a lot of what I had, I think," Nadia said. "It's a Romanian thing. She's very, very ambitious."[1]

Dominique was promoted on television shows, magazine covers, and newspaper articles as the next Nadia. "The comparisons with Nadia and I are really good for me," Dominique said. "Our styles are a little different, but I think it's nice to be compared to the best. It's really neat that it's the twenty-year anniversary for Nadia, and we look alike, and maybe it's time for another one to come up. And hopefully I can get some gold medals, too."

Bela could see many similarities between the two. "The way they are fighting out on the floor, the aggressive way of performing—yeah, that's identical," he allowed.

Dominique was also compared with Bela's other Olympic champion. "I like to be compared to Nadia and Mary Lou," Dominique admitted. "I think it's because I have the personality of Mary Lou and some of the styles of Nadia, and so it's a combination of both. I enjoy it, personally."

While Dominique liked the comparisons, she wanted to leave her own mark on gymnastics. "I'm my own person, too," she reminded everyone, "and I want to show everybody my own personality and my new style, because I'm Dominique and I'm a different person. I want to show everybody what I can do [so they will] remember me like they remembered Nadia."

"Can she be the next Nadia?" Bela asked. "She will never be the next Nadia. Nadia was one, and that's it. But she can be the first Dominique, and that would create again a great, lovely, and very, very alive idol for thousands of our young people. She will be Dominique Moceanu and not Nadia."

It seemed fitting that Bela's coaching career, which had started with a dark-haired Romanian, now ended with another ponytailed brunette of Romanian heritage. "She is the one who really lights up our late coaching career," Bela said. "She's a smiling, communicative, young individual—the one whose little mouth is non-stop saying something, commenting on something—with ups and downs."

With all the comparisons to two former Olympic champions, it was not surprising that Dominique was also touted as America's best hope for gold at the Olympics. Although Shannon Miller and Dominique Dawes were past Olympians and more accomplished than Dominique, the press had cast the two veterans aside for the excitement of a more vibrant, youthful star ever since Dominique's 1995 U.S. Championship victory.

Dominique seemed unfazed by the pressure. "I just go with the flow," she said with a smile. "I just do my stuff." When asked about being a performer, she said, "I guess it's just natural for me. I love being out there in front of the crowd and showing all my abilities, and everybody looking up at you and having fun."

"She feels no pressure," Nadia surmised. "She shows the consistency of her training, because she has done each routine many, many times until they are perfect."[2]

Still, Bela felt the need to shield his young charge from the press and other distractions so that she could remain focused. As the Olympics approached, he barred the media from workouts except on designated media days when television crews and reporters were allowed in the gym. They did not distract Dominique too much since she had grown accustomed to their frequent visits. The journalists were not allowed to disrupt workouts, although Bela had his gymnasts do fewer routines than normal so they would have time to answer questions. Sometimes, reporters would hide outside the gym on non-media days and approach gymnasts as they were leaving.

"He did a good job of trying to keep the pressure off of us,"

Betty Okino remembered about her Olympic experience, "because he'd keep us away from all the media even to the last day before the Olympics. He only let us do one or two interviews and those were necessary interviews. The rest of the time he kept the media away from us, and us away from the media, so we didn't have to get all caught up in it."

Dominique thrived in Bela's program because she, her parents, and her coaches were all like-minded. Her development had been influenced by the same Romanian heritage to which Bela was accustomed. Her strict parents had provided Dominique with an upbringing different from that of most American children, whom they believed to be somewhat pampered. They thought nothing of the hard work and long hours in the gym. That was what made Dominique successful; that was what brought results. Everyone was in agreement and able to work together toward a common goal: bringing home the Olympic gold.

While an Olympic medal was within reach, Dominique tried to keep everything in perspective. She knew how well things had been going for Kim Zmeskal when disaster had struck.

"[Kim has] told me a couple of times about her experiences," Dominique said. "She's told me, 'Don't worry about it. Bela's here to support you. You just have to do your routines like you do them and don't worry about anything else.' I give her a call sometimes and she helps me out. She's a really good friend."

Kim tried to be an encouragement to her young colleague. "Hopefully, she learned from me that no matter what happens, as long as you're enjoying what you're doing as you're doing it, it will all be okay in the end," Kim said. "People always talk about the pressure and how you're training your whole life for one moment. Hopefully, she realizes that all these experiences that she's going through right now make all of it worth it no matter what happens."

Dominique wanted to make the Olympic team and win the all-around with all her heart, but she was realistic enough to recognize her dream was not a sure thing. "Well, if it doesn't work out, that's life and you have to go on," she said softly, as though fate might be listening. "But we're all hoping and praying that we'll go straight forward and make it all the way."

As the Games approached, Dominique's workouts at the ranch became tougher and her schedule more demanding. She woke up at 6:50 A.M.—usually without the help of an alarm clock, although she set two of them just in case. Then she grabbed a quick breakfast of fruit, a bran muffin, and some juice before walking over to the gym.

Her first workout was from 7:30 to 11:30. Afterwards she ate a lunch specially prepared for her and Kerri which usually consisted of grilled chicken, rice, and steamed vegetables. Then she watched *Days of our Lives* from 1:00 to 2:00 P.M. The soap opera helped to get her mind off gymnastics. In the afternoon she napped and did physical therapy, which included ultrasound or a massage for an hour.

Bela wanted her to rest when she was not in the gym. He did not like her spending too much time laying in the sun at the pool or playing volleyball since those activities zapped her energy. But relaxing was difficult because the ranch was always bustling with campers who wanted to talk to her or get an autograph.

In the evening it was back to the gym from 4:00 until 7:30. After a dinner of Apple Jacks or Corn Pops cereal, she relaxed from her exhausting day and went to sleep by 10:30. In about eight hours she would get up and do it all over again.

The increase in workout intensity meant more repetitions in the gym. She did ten to fifteen optional and compulsory beam routines, six to ten sets on uneven bars, two to four floor routines, and twelve to twenty of each vault.

Since there were no foam pits at the ranch gym, she had to endure added pounding on her body. Her right shin began bothering her, but thinking it was only a pulled muscle, she did not become overly concerned. Bela expected her to be tough and push through minor injuries, so she ignored it.

"Just bite your teeth and do it," Dominique thought to herself. "It's just a muscle."

Bela certainly did not baby his athletes. "We are not in the gym to be having fun," he had once observed. "The fun comes in the end, with the winning and the medals. Sometimes the preparation is so hard, so intense. They are crying. They are screaming. It is over the top."[3]

Nadia knew what Bela meant. "If somebody is thinking that winning an Olympic medal is not hard work," she said, "this is wrong."

"We are not fooling around," Bela reiterated. "There is no such thing as playing around, because [gymnastics is] the most disciplined sport in the world."

Hilary Grivich, a gymnast who had been through the Olympic pressure cooker, explained, "The mentality is different because you know what you're preparing for. What you've been working for this whole long time all these years is coming down to just a couple weeks or months. Your own mentality changes, and everyone else's around you becomes more intense."

"You can feel the pressure when you walk in the gym," Betty elaborated.

Dominique and Kerri knew time was short. "We're all aware that there's just a little while longer, so you need to make each workout productive," Kerri said. "There's no time to be wasted."

"I try not to think about the pressure all the time," Dominique said. "If you have a goal in gymnastics and you want to

127

achieve it, you have to have ambition. Everything is going to take hard work in life. You have to know what your goals are and work hard to achieve them."[4]

She was not one to shy away from hard work. She did not complain about the long hours, nor was she concerned about missing out on things other kids her age were doing. She was doing what she wanted to do. The work was difficult, but she knew it would benefit her later.

"All this hard work in gymnastics will pay off," Dominique said seriously. "Push really hard now and then all the rest of the years I'll be *free* and I can do whatever I want."

She was glad to have Kerri in the gym with her. They were both going through the same things in practice every day, and both wanted to do well at the Olympics. When one of them was struggling, the other yelled, "Come on, you can do it!"

After so many grueling training sessions, Bela's athletes were in top form and ready to make a statement at the U.S. Championships in Knoxville, Tennessee. Both were determined to claim top spots.

The pre-Olympic media hype in Tennessee was a constant distraction for Dominique. Everywhere she turned, people posed questions, asked for her signature, or wanted something.

"The media is a big problem at some of the events," John Geddert observed. "I know that the cameras in the face must be distracting to the athletes. . . . Many of the media try to interview when *they* want to. This can be very distracting, but getting press is important, so we put up with them."

On Wednesday, June 5, Dominique began the defense of her national title. She had a solid competition in compulsories, scoring a 9.80 on vault, a 9.75 on bars, a 9.825 on beam, and a 9.875 on floor. However, Shannon was slightly better and finished first.

To advance to the Olympic Trials, Dominique merely needed to stay in the top fourteen. Barring a major catastrophe, she would easily make the cut, but she was also hoping to retain her crown.

Like last year, Dominique began optionals on vault and Shannon began on beam. Also like last year, Shannon fell on a back layout somersault, leaving the door open for Dominique.

Bela gave her some final instructions as he massaged her right leg. While preparing for the Knoxville showdown, her leg had begun hurting more and more. She had tried to shake it off at first but soon realized it was more serious.

"I really started to feel sharp pain," Dominique said, "and then that's when I knew something was wrong with it."

Bela and Marta wondered if Dominique should continue competing. "They asked me how I was feeling," she said. "It hurt, but what could I do? I had to finish my competition. I had to bite my teeth somehow and make it through. It was really bad at first."

To get through the meet, Dominique took pain killers, tightly taped her leg and heel, and gutted it out. She walked up the stairs to the vault podium, clenched her teeth, and pulled out two solid vaults. The highest score, a 9.75, counted. But Jaycie Phelps outshined both Dominique and Shannon in the first round with a superb bar routine that earned her the early lead.

On bars, Dominique ran into trouble on the free hip circle after her Pak salto. Her hips were way too close to the low bar and she could not execute the move properly. The rest of the set was clean, but she took a few steps on her dismount. Disappointed, she walked over to Bela and waited to hear what she already knew.

Bela put it bluntly: "That was no good, Domi. That was no

good." He then told her to find a place to warm up for the next event. She quickly took off her grips and wrist bands and headed over to beam, hardly noticing the 9.55 on the scoreboard.

Dominique bravely fought her way back into contention on the wooden apparatus. She was aggressive and confident, scoring a 9.80. While she opted for conservative tumbling on floor to protect her ailing leg, her playful new routine to *"Devil Went Down to Georgia"* had the spectators clapping their hands and stomping their feet. When she finished, the stands erupted with fans waving tens on sticks like overanxious bidders at an auction.

Bela and Marta showed their approval with warm hugs. They seemed to think the routine might put her on top in the standings, but NBC commentator Tim Daggett remarked, "It was a great routine, but I just don't think it's going to be quite enough to overtake Jaycie and Shannon. I think she needed to do the bigger first tumbling pass."

When the score, a 9.80, was posted, Dominique stared in disbelief. She wound up third behind Shannon—who had staged a remarkable comeback to win even after a fall on beam—and Jaycie. Dominique was disappointed with the outcome. As other athletes congratulated her, she forced a smile and mumbled an insincere thanks. She then tried to leave the arena, but the television cameras and reporters followed, not wanting to miss an opportunity to ask inane questions about her disappointing performance.

"It was exciting coming back to Nationals and competing optionals and everything," she said woodenly. "It was a good practice meet for the upcoming events, and hopefully it will get better. I'm looking forward to Trials. . . . Everyone wants to be at the top. Everybody is working hard. It's a fight up there."

At the press conference after the meet, Dominique did not mention her leg injury as an excuse for the lackluster showing.

Also not wanting to draw attention to Dominique's ailing leg, Bela focused on her bruised heel, saying, "Skills, altitude, take-offs—all were affected" by it. "She's not in 100% shape," he added. "You can imagine—[it's as if] you don't have a foot."

Dominique's sullen countenance was in stark contrast to her usual public image, and some speculated this meet marked the end of her honeymoon with the media. In addition to inquiries about her performance, she had to answer increasingly negative questions about whether she was too young for such a demanding lifestyle. It was ironic that Shannon, only four-and-a-half years Dominique's senior, was constantly told she was too old while Dominique faced charges that she was too young.

"I love this sport, and I'm doing what I have to do for me," Dominique countered. "But some people just don't get it. I'm not losing my childhood. I have the rest of my life to have a childhood."[5]

The event finals were held Saturday. Dominique warmed up her events but decided at the last minute not to compete. Shannon, Jaycie, and Amanda Borden all withdrew from the finals as well. Needless to say, the 10,000 fans were very disappointed. Explaining to the audience her reason for not participating, each gymnast said she was suffering from nagging injuries and wanted to give her body a break. With the top four out, Dominique Dawes won every event.

Dominique looked forward to going home. She admitted feeling like she had competed on one leg at Nationals. There were only a few weeks until the Olympic Trials, and with or without injuries she had a lot of preparation ahead of her. Despite the urgency, Bela allowed her to rest for two days.

On Dominique's first day back in the gym, Bela realized something was seriously wrong with her leg. "On the very first

131

dismount, she collapsed on the ground, which I didn't know what to think," he stated. "I said, 'Domi, you can't do that. You can hurt yourself if you just let yourself fall.' She did not say a word. On the second attempt, she fell just like her legs gave up, and I said, 'Stop!' "

Dominique went to the doctor and learned after a magnetic resonance imaging (MRI) that she had a stress fracture four centimeters long in her mid-tibia. The doctors noticed the inflammation of the bone and warned that her leg could snap in half if she continued to press it. They strongly urged that she stay off it as much as possible during workouts—no landings or heavy pressure—until July 7, which was over three weeks away.

Dominique burst into tears. "How can this happen right now?" she cried.

Bela was upset as well. "It was bad," he said gravely. "We had to face reality and the pretty dramatic MRI pictures. She saw them. It was nothing you could really cheer yourself up about."

The diagnosis was sobering. "A lot of doctors looked at her, and everybody agreed it was bad," Bela admitted. "It's hard to say what's going to happen now. The only thing we can do is wait. It's going to be excruciating. The worst part is she's still a kid. She doesn't understand everything, and she's very down."[6]

Several factors had apparently contributed to her injury. She had first noticed some discomfort in the spring when she began overcompensating with her right leg for the heel injury that plagued her left. Out of necessity, she had forced her right leg to pick up the slack until her heel rehabilitated. The resulting injury had been further aggravated by the lack of soft landing surfaces, such as foam pits, at the ranch.

Dominique had two options: she could continue to prepare for Trials and risk further injury, or she could rest and save herself for the Olympics. The decision seemed simple, but the real question was whether she could skip the Trials and still make the team.

Ever the master strategist, Bela knew how to play the political game and win. He had been burned by the system at the last Olympic Trials in 1992 and was determined not to let that happen again. Dominique was one of the top-ranked gymnasts in the country and thus virtually guaranteed a spot on the team. Bela banked on this when he submitted a petition to USA Gymnastics with a medical form signed by a doctor citing a stress fracture in Dominique's leg as the reason she could not compete. He was taking a gamble, however, because if the petition were not approved, Dominique would not be allowed to compete at Trials and thus be disqualified from the selection process.

Dominique was not the only athlete taking this risk. Shannon did the same thing because of a wrist injury. Bela and Steve Nunno hoped that Dominique and Shannon, because of their accomplishments, could skip Trials and be put directly on the Olympic team.

The official USA Gymnastics Olympic team selection procedures stated, "If one of the top seven gymnasts in rank order from National Championships is injured after the National Championships, her injury is verified by a physician approved by USA Gymnastics, and the petition is then accepted, her National Championships' score will be her score for Olympic Trials. This score is entered into the all-around results prior to the start of the Olympic Trials. If her total score from National Championships remains within the top seven ranked all-around scores from Trials, she has earned one of the seven slots on the Olympic team."

After receiving the petitions, a four-person committee gathered to decided the fate of these two athletes. The next day, USA Gymnastics announced that it would allow Dominique and

Shannon to use their scores from the U.S. Championships in place of ones from the Trials.

Dominique received the news with mixed emotions. She was happy they had accepted the petition, but she was a little concerned since she had not had the best showing at Championships. Though it seemed unlikely that six other gymnasts would outdo her mark of 78.22, it was always a possibility, especially since scores tended to improve by about a point, on average, at Trials.

"I want to try and keep her mood up, but this is very hard," Bela said worriedly. "We don't know how her scores are going to hold up. It's tough on her. We all have worked a long time, and then this. But these are things that happen."[7]

"This thing had to happen now and I don't know why it did," Dominique anguished. "This is my dream to go to the Olympics and I can't do anything about it." Pausing, she covered her eyes and cried silently for a few moments. After regaining her composure, she added, "All my work will be down the drain and I won't be for sure on the team. I've been working all my life for this, so it's really hard on me right now."

Four years ago, nearly the same thing had happened to Kim. A few weeks before the Olympics, she had developed a stress fracture in her left leg that forced her to remove her most difficult tumbling passes and caused her scores to suffer. Dominique did not want her Olympic dream to slip away like Kim's had done because of an injury she could not control.

To combat the injury, Dominique began an intense program of physical therapy. She strapped an Exogen Bone Accelerator directly on the injured area three times a day for twenty minutes to stimulate the bone with low-intensity ultrasonic waves. She also took vitamins and tried to get as much sleep as possible to speed the healing process.

Missing the Olympics was out of the question. "I *have* to be there," she stressed. "I *want* to be there. I'm training and doing everything I can to get it healed as soon as possible. . . . That's all I can do is pray that they'll let me go on the team. I want them to know I'm training and doing everything possible."

Bela adopted a training method for Dominique that had worked very well for Mary Lou after her knee surgery only a few weeks before the 1984 Olympics. Bela made Dominique ride a stationary bike while her floor music played. She pedaled normally and did the arm movements to the dance parts of her floor routine then pedaled furiously in place of her tumbling passes. Dominique did not think it was that difficult the first time, but after Bela made her do several run-throughs in a row, she was exhausted. The exercise helped maintain her endurance without aggravating her injury.

"I've done a lot of bicycle and a lot of conditioning to keep up my strength," she told reporters. "That's the most important—you have to have a lot of physical strength. It will be easier to come back when you're stronger and better than before."

Of the other three events, vaulting was a definite no-no. Dominique could do some beam and bars but no dismounts. She had to be careful, though, since falling off the equipment could reinjure her leg.

The *Today* show came out to the ranch to do a feature on Dominique and her struggles. She acknowledged how difficult the next two weeks were going to be as she awaited the results of both the Olympic Trials and her own private battle.

Dominique was disappointed that she could not compete in Boston, as were the people who had bought their tickets to the Trials specifically to see her and Shannon before the Olympics. Although the two athletes came to watch the meet, their nonperformance at the competition elicited criticism of USA Gymnastics for consistently coming up with a questionable team selection process that was always fraught with controversy. The sport's governing body seemed to change the process every four years while keeping it only slightly less complicated than the U.S. tax code.

In 1984, two meets, the U.S. Championships and the Olympic Trials, had been used to pick the top eight gymnasts. The top four athletes made the team automatically while the remaining four went to a training camp where two alternates would be decided. Kathy Johnson, in eighth place after a 7.65 on her compulsory bar routine, was given the nod to compete ahead of Lucy Wener, fifth, and Marie Roethlisberger, seventh. Because Lucy had done so well at both meets yet still had not made the team, the decision caused a bit of a stir.

Four years later in 1988, USA Gymnastics caved to criticism and based the team on the top six scores from the U.S. Championships and the Trials, with seventh and eighth place earning the alternate spots. When 1987 U.S. Champion Kristie Phillips had a bad meet and wound up eighth, she was not given preferential treatment or a second chance like Kathy Johnson had received four years earlier. Thus, questions arose about whether the best team had been fielded.

Low and behold, the Olympic team selection process changed again to avoid controversy in 1992. However, the new process backfired severely and even resulted in a lawsuit against USA Gymnastics. The team was decided after several grueling meets. First there was the U.S. Championships, then the Olympic Trials, and finally a private meet in Orlando. Kim Kelly, who had finished sixth at Trials, was the unlucky person not chosen for the Olympic team during a secretive, backroom selection meeting of the coaches. Wendy Bruce, who had finished seventh, was placed ahead of her, as was Betty Okino, who did not compete at either the Championships or the Trials. Kim Kelly was so upset she filed suit.

No surprise in 1996, instead of making a small change like eliminating the private meet, USA Gymnastics decided to revamp the entire system and count only the scores from the Trials. With this new method, a relatively unknown gymnast could have an outstanding meet and bump off a veteran performer who happened to have a really bad day.

There had to be a solution that balanced the process and accomplished its goal: to choose the best team. One meet was not the answer, but neither were secret meetings between coaches. Besides, almost every elite gymnast struggled with injuries, and that fact needed to fit into the equation.

Bela thought the best way to select the team was to hand pick the top athletes without a meet. He knew this would never happen in the United States, so the Eastern European countries that chose their squads this way would always have an advantage.

Dominique arrived in Boston on Wednesday night. Thursday and Friday she went to the FleetCenter for a light workout in the competition arena. Friday evening, she marched in and was presented with the other gymnasts. She received a warm greeting, smiled and waved to the screaming fans, then left the competition floor and joined her family in a private box.

It was difficult to watch from the sidelines. "I really wanted to be out there competing," Dominique said.

From the moment the first gymnast landed her vault, it was clear the scores were not going to be higher than they had been at Nationals. In fact, some eyebrow-raising low marks caused observers to wonder whether the scores for lesser-known gymnasts were being kept deliberately low. It seemed that perhaps the team had been chosen long ago—at least the top spots—and barring any major mistakes, the Trials were a mere formality.

"It's obviously not the same scoring system that they used at Nationals," Kelli Hill openly charged. "It's being done to protect the two petitioners."

Dominique soon realized the scores would not be enough to unseat her. "We had it all figured out," she said. "My mom had the calculator, and I was doing it mentally, too. After the first couple of rotations, we knew. Then I started looking forward to Atlanta."

By the end of the evening it was announced by Bela and confirmed by USA Gymnastics that Dominique had made the team. Even if all the other athletes scored perfect tens in optionals, Dominique's position in the top seven was secure.

On Sunday afternoon, Dominique went through a very light workout, doing mostly stretching exercises. Shortly before the meet was scheduled to begin, she stopped and began to change clothes. As she discreetly slipped off her leotard from under her T-shirt, some fans called out her name. She waved from underneath her shirt, which drew a few laughs. Then she donned her USA warmup suit and sat on the men's parallel bars podium chatting with Shannon. Like the two of them, this podium would not see any action this evening since the men had finished competing on Saturday.

After the march-in, she again went to a skybox to watch the meet with her family. She was more relaxed this time since she knew she had made the team. She sipped on a drink and talked to Shannon. Although the two were not performing, they were acknowledged by the audience when shown on the big screen in the FleetCenter. One fan brought a sign that read "We miss you, Shannon and Dominique."

The other athletes battled it out for the remaining five spots. When the chalk cleared, veterans Dominique Dawes and Kerri Strug had clawed their way to the top. Jaycie Phelps, Amy

Chow, and Amanda Borden had also reserved positions. Dominique was happy with the team selection, but she was sad to see that her friend Jennie Thompson had not made it.

Bela was also pleased with the final results. "This is the strongest team ever," he exulted. "I don't ever remember having such a talented group of gymnasts on the floor. These girls are contenders for medals, and plenty of them."

The sellout crowd of over 17,000 cheered wildly as the seven members were announced during the awards ceremony. USA Gymnastics appointed Marta the team's head coach and Mary Lee Tracy, the coach of Amanda and Jaycie, the assistant. This was the first time in forty years an all-female staff had been selected.

Kathy Scanlan, president of USA Gymnastics, explained, "Because [the Karolyis] have an athlete who is unable to compete here because of injury, and because she needs some really intense training before the Olympics, we thought it was in the best interests of the team to have Bela work exclusively with Dominique."

Marta was startled by the choice. "When she called me into the room, I thought they were going to ask me where Bela was so they could tell him he was going to be head coach," she said. "When they asked if I wanted to be the coach, of course I was surprised. But of course I *had* to say yes."[8]

Bela considered it a slap in the face not to be asked. He knew Marta was an excellent coach, but he was quick to put the pressure on her, saying, "You better do a good job."

The day after the Trials, the *Today* show asked Dominique back for a follow up to its story of a few weeks ago. Then she returned to the ranch, although she could not resume her full training for another week. There for only a few days after the Trials, she had just enough time to unpack and repack for the Olympics. Since she would be gone about a month, she had to take a lot of leotards.

As she filled her suitcase with everything she would need in the upcoming weeks, Dominique could not help but wonder how her leg would hold up when she resumed full training. "It's going to be a tough fight out there," she acknowledged. "I have to go out and do all my routines next week. Bela would do anything to help me out, and I'm greatly appreciative of what he does for me. It's been really great having him as a coach."

"She believes in me, and that's the hardest on me," Bela said as tears welled up in his eyes. "She looks up at me and I see the little brown eyes, big and wide. My heart is breaking because I know what's going on in her mind: 'Bela, help me.'

"If I could give part of my leg, I would do it in this particular situation. It probably is a stupid statement, but I would really help any way I could with this kid at this moment. It's breaking my heart." He paused to wipe away a tear. "I love her. Yes, I do love her."

Dominique hoped her leg would be strong and the Olympic coaches would not see any reason to dismiss her from the team. "This has been my dream and everything," she reiterated. "You have to prepare yourself for the worst, and hopefully pray for the best. So we'll see."

Dominique had the mettle to endure this crisis and come out on top. It would not be easy, but she could do it. Still, her predicament reminded everyone that, for all her toughness and determination, she was, after all, an innocent young girl.

"She's still the one who thinks the world is made up of sugar and she's climbing the sugar mountain," Bela said. "At the top of the sugar mountain there is going to be the sunshine. Gosh, I wish all her life would be the same. But I think and I know there would be a deep scar on her mind and her heart for the rest of her life if this thing would go the wrong way."

Chapter 9

Quest for Gold

A fter a month off, Dominique resumed full workouts on July 7. "The floor and the vault are the ones that I have to do now," she said excitedly. "I have to do some of the beam and lots of other little things."

Dominique tightly wrapped her leg with a bandage, gritted her teeth, and began the task of making a comeback. Her leg still hurt but not as much as before. Her doctors said the bone was thickening, which meant it was getting stronger.

"The leg is better," she stated. "It's healing, but it's not fully going to be healed until after the Olympics. So there's going to be a little pain, but it's not dangerous."

With only two weeks until the big show, Dominique needed to be focused like never before. "I know what I have to do," she said matter-of-factly. "I have [to be] consistent in training. Marta and Bela know what they have to do with me. They're always there to support me and guide me all the way."

Not surprisingly, critics questioned whether pushing Dominique's injury was worth it. If she continued, she could break her leg. Dominique, her parents, and her coaches brushed off this worst-case scenario and focused on how much progress she had made in such a short time. Dominique never wanted to look back and wonder what might have been if only she had tried to compete. Waiting four more years for the next Olympics seemed like an eternity. She was at her prime now and desperately wanted to be a contender.

"It's the Olympics," she said emphatically. "It's my dream. I've always wanted to be there and I'm going to make myself be there no matter what."

Only two days after resuming full training, Dominique and her coaches flew to Greensboro, North Carolina, the site of the training camp for the women's gymnastics team. For several days the Olympic squad polished their routines at the Greensboro Coliseum on equipment similar to that being used in the Games. Besides adjusting to working as a team, the group adapted to the Eastern time zone and the warm climate.

Friday, July 12, was media day. "My recovery is going really well," Dominique told reporters. "I'm doing a lot better than I was. There's still a little pain there, and there's going to be a little bit, but the doctors said it's okay and it's getting better. I just have to be strong and pull through."

The training camp concluded the following day with an exhibition at the Coliseum. Dominique competed on all four events, but to protect her leg she did the compulsory floor routine instead of her optional set and landed the other three events on heavily-padded mats. Still, she was satisfied with her performances. She nailed her vault and hit her new bar dismount, a full-twisting double layout.

After the exhibition, the media scurried over to ask the usual leg-related questions. Dominique looked tiredly into the camera and rattled off her stock answer: "There's still some pain there and there's *always* going to be a little bit there, but I'll just have to be strong and tough and deal with it."

The team traveled to Atlanta the next day. When they arrived at the airport, Dominique and Bela obliged the local press with a few words before heading for accreditation, where they received their athletic badges. Worn around their necks, these credentials allowed access into restricted areas like the Olympic Village. Dominique was also measured for her Olympic uniform, jacket, and ring, which she would receive later. The entire process took a good seven hours, but she whiled away the time by rummaging through the neat stuff she received in her goody bag, like clothes and a Cabbage Patch doll.

Around 9:00 P.M., the team checked into its secret lodging facility, a fraternity house at Emory University called Connally House. Security guards protected the two-story brick building around the clock, while inside the gymnasts enjoyed luxurious furniture, multiple televisions, and individual bedrooms. The private enclave also included such amenities as nutritionists, sports psychologists, and chefs. In past years the team had stayed in the Olympic Village, but problems with noise and distractions had convinced the coaches to board the athletes in a more isolated spot.

Besides living in protected seclusion, the team trained in a private club at an undisclosed location while all of the other gymnasts practiced at the Atlanta International Convention Center near the airport. The U.S. women wanted to work out at the same time of day that their meets would be held, and it was not possible to do that at the Convention Center.

This special treatment brought sharp criticism from other countries. "It's not fair," Romanian head coach Octavian Belu protested, noting that the Spanish team had trained with all the other competitors at the 1992 Barcelona Games. "Why don't they train with us?" He felt the opportunity to "train in secret" gave the Americans an unfair advantage.

"It's not meant to be anything of an advantage," maintained Kathy Kelly, women's program director for USA Gymnastics. "We are not training any more hours a day than is set up by the organizing committee."

Just before the start of the Games there were two podium workouts—one for compulsories and one for optionals—in the Georgia Dome, which had been divided in half to accommodate basketball on the other side. The podium practices helped the gymnasts get acquainted with their surroundings and get used to competing on elevated equipment.

Fans paid up to $22.00 each to see the gymnastics practice sessions. More than 30,000 sports enthusiasts showed up to watch the gymnasts work out, and Dominique enjoyed an early taste of what it was like to have the home advantage. The crowd cheered wildly for anything the U.S. athletes did.

Dominique tried to keep a low profile when not practicing, but the press was scrambling to get as many interviews as possible. "I really want to do the best that I can, because this has been my dream," she told reporters. "I've always wanted to be in the Olympics, and now that I'm here, I want to show everybody what I can do."

Although the media hype was intense, Bela thought Dominique could handle it. "The pressure and expectation thing is coming on and on and on," he said, "and, of course, the media is exaggerating it. Well, there is pressure, but it's not . . . a destroying, squeezing, torturing feeling. No, it's an anxiousness to go into the competition."

The excitement began in earnest Friday night, July 19, with the opening ceremonies. Dominique found the spectacular display inspiring even though she and her teammates had to watch it on television. Since they would have had to stand out in the heat and humidity for at least four hours, the coaches had decided it was better not to go and risk getting sick or worn down.

The ceremonies made Dominique feel very patriotic. While she loved her Romanian heritage and had a special place in her heart for Nadia and the Romanian team, she was red-white-and-blue through and through.

For the past year, Dominique had been counting the days until the Olympics using a homemade calendar on her bedroom wall. Now there were no more days left. Looking back, the time seemed to have gone by so quickly, yet growing up the Olympics had always seemed like a distant dream. Now the dream was becoming a reality.

"I'm not really scared," she stated. "I'm more anxious and excited about it because this is the *Olympics.* . . . I'm looking forward to competing. There's going to be a full crowd. It's sold out. It's a once-in-a-lifetime opportunity. Who knows when they'll come back here? This is perfect timing for me: the age limit I just made, Bela just came back, and the Olympics are here. I feel like this is my time. I want to do it."

Dominique hoped her eleven years of preparation would be enough. She also hoped her leg would hold up. At least it was comforting to know other great gymnasts had faced adversity like this just before the Games and still come out on top. Shannon had dislocated her elbow three months before the 1992 Olympics in Barcelona where she won an unprecedented five medals. Mary Lou had undergone knee surgery a little over a month before the

1984 Games, and Nadia had competed in 1976 with a badly-sprained ankle. Both had won the all-around gold.

Dominique wanted to win it all like Mary Lou had done twelve years prior, but she was shrewd enough not to pin all her hopes on gold alone, at least not publicly. "I hope to win any medal," she said. "I really want to hit my routines and do the best that I can. I can do a medal if I do that. First comes hitting my routines and doing my best."

Medaling would not be easy. A Soviet boycott of the 1984 Olympics had given Mary Lou an advantage Dominique would not have. Nonetheless, Mary Lou remained a firm believer in Dominique's potential.

"Dominique Moceanu definitely has the ability to do big this summer in Atlanta," she declared enthusiastically. "She is so much fun to watch. Her gymnastics is incredible."

At age fourteen, Dominique was the shortest and lightest member of the U.S. contingent. She was also one of the youngest athletes competing in Atlanta. If she had been born a few months later, she would not have been allowed to participate. A gymnast had to have her fifteenth birthday sometime during the year of the Olympics to be eligible to compete. This rule was later changed so that, beginning with the 2000 Games, a gymnast had to turn sixteen in the Olympic year.

The format of the Olympics was the same as that of the World Championships. The first part was the team compulsories and the second was team optionals. Whichever team had the highest total after both competitions won. The third part, the all-around final, decided the best individual gymnast. In the fourth and final part, event finals, gymnasts competed individually on only those events for which they had qualified by finishing among the top eight in the team competition.

The women's compulsories were Sunday, July 21. The U.S.,

after a random draw, began on uneven bars in the third of four sessions. This was a good starting position. Romania had the misfortune of drawing the first session, where scores tended to be lower, while Russia and China drew the most advantageous fourth and final session.

Dominique preferred starting on bars, so she was happy with the rotation order. Since beam followed bars, this rotation allowed the gymnasts to get the two most nerve-wracking events behind them early so they could be more relaxed on floor and vault.

The U.S. women—faces deadly serious, determination burning fiercely in their eyes—marched in under a barrage of cheers. They were armed with hand grips and ready for battle. Dominique made sure her grips were securely in place as she prepared for the three-minute touch warmup. Not wanting to take any unnecessary risks, she had rubber bands wrapped tightly around her fingers to make sure the grips stayed in place.

Dominique had a rocky touch warmup. She fell twice attempting her hecht and did not even get to try a dismount. While her leg still ached, she was more concerned about her problems in the warmup than with her injury.

Kerri Strug, Jaycie Phelps, Amy Chow, and Dominique Dawes started the competition strongly for the Americans. Dominique quelled her nerves to pull out a solid routine for a 9.725, and Shannon capped off the event with an excellent set.

The team was focused. They usually did not congratulate each other after a good routine, nor did they watch each other's sets. Once an athlete finished her routine, she immediately began practicing on the sidelines for the next event. Some said the team lacked unity, but it was impossible to deny the Americans' intense drive and concentration.

The next event did not go as smoothly. Wobbly routines on

beam from Kerri, Amanda, and Dominique Dawes were followed by a fall from Jaycie. The pressure was on Shannon and Dominique. Both needed extraordinary sets to pull the U.S. team out of the hole it had dug for itself. Fortunately, they were equal to the challenge. Shannon coolly logged a 9.737, the highest score on the event, while Dominique calmly and confidently executed a routine worth a 9.687.

On floor, Jaycie, Dominique Dawes, and Amanda danced expressively to earn solid scores. Dominique was clean for a 9.75. Shannon and Kerri were outstanding and pulled their team ahead of the Romanians—who had gone earlier in the day—for the first time.

The final event was the vault. Jaycie started them off well. Dominique was second and earned a 9.662 with only a slight shuffle on the landing.

"Good, good," Bela said as he leaned over the barrier to give her a hug. Only the head coach and the assistant coach for each team were allowed on the floor; the rest of the U.S. entourage had to stand behind a wall with the reporters and photographers. "All right, it's over now. You can relax."

The remaining four gymnasts nailed their Tsukahara vaults to propel the U.S. well ahead of Romania and into the lead for the moment. However, the Chinese and Russians were still to come in the final round, and scores tended to rise a little higher with each session.

Bela embraced his wife and told her what a good coaching job she had done. He also hugged Steve Nunno, who now seemed more like a friend than a rival. Meanwhile, Mary Lee Tracy gathered the team together for a brief meeting.

"We're all going to turn around to the crowd and yell 'USA! USA!'—okay?" she said. "Everybody try it. Get your arms up and make the crowd get into it. But we've got to hold off until everyone's done competing."

After the final competitor finished on floor, the women turned to the audience and began chanting the patriotic mantra. The American fans immediately picked up on it, and the refrain echoed throughout the Georgia Dome. People rose to their feet to acknowledge the athletes as they took a lap around the arena.

In the final compulsory round, the Chinese had problems on bars and beam that effectively dropped them out of contention. The Russians, however, took full advantage of their fourth-round draw to surpass the United States by a little over a tenth and grab the top spot.

The Romanians, who had been favored to win, were in third after compulsories. Regrettably, they had arrived in Atlanta already demoralized from the loss of three strong athletes— Andrea Cacovean, Claudia Presecan, and Nadia Hatagan—who had suffered injuries before the Games. Their problems had continued when Ana Maria Bican injured her knee at a training session in Atlanta and had to have surgery, leaving only six able-bodied team members with no time to fly in a replacement. But not even these six were completely healthy. Gina Gogean had almost decided not to compete because of an emergency appendectomy a few weeks prior, and Lavinia Milosovici was competing on an injured ankle.

"[The U.S.] looked like a very strong army," Octavian Belu remarked after the meet, "and we looked like a commando unit trying to survive."[1]

The Americans looked strong, but they were by no means free of injuries. Besides Dominique's stress fracture, Shannon was still nursing a wrist injury and Amy suffered from pain in her lower back.

"The adrenaline that's running through your body helps you get over any pain you might be feeling," Dominique said in response to inquiries about her leg at a press conference after the meet. "Sure, I can feel it from time to time when I'm warming up or when I'm walking around, but you just get a mind-set that it's not going to hurt. When you start to compete, especially in front of a crowd like that, it all goes away."

Dominique was fifth overall in the individual standings and hoped to improve her position during the optionals. A day separated the two competitions during which the men finished their team competition and the women fine-tuned their sets.

At 3:00 P.M. on Tuesday, Dominique began her warmup for the team final. Led by team captain Amanda, the group jogged in a circle around the blue floor mat. As they warmed up in the practice gym on the side of the arena, the third-round teams competed. These four squads—China, Hungary, Belarus, and Spain—would most likely not win medals since they were not in the final. Only the top four teams after compulsories were allowed to compete in the final, which provided a big scoring advantage. Dominique could hear scattered applause from the predominantly-American crowd, who waited anxiously for the real showdown to begin. She hoped her team could fulfill the hopes and expectations of this biased audience.

Dominique tried not to think about the pressure as she skipped, hopped, jogged, and circled her arms in unison with her teammates. When they finished their initial exercises, the gymnasts disbursed and each found her personal coach to continue warming up. Dominique sat on the floor, leaned forward, and touched her toes while Marta pushed on her back until her stomach touched her legs. Bela worked with Kerri the same way.

Stretching was followed by beam skills practiced on the floor. Since the general warmup had not started, all four teams shared the forty-foot by forty-foot mat. It was amazing that no one crashed into another competitor. Front flips and back handsprings were being thrown on every square foot of the blue carpet. Each team, while pretending the others did not exist, was trying to intimidate its opponents.

The U.S. women began their first of four fifteen-minute warmup rotations on the beam. They ended the general warmup on bars, their first competitive event of the evening. Afterwards, they quickly gathered their belongings and lined up to march in.

When the Americans emerged for the first time, fans leaped to their feet waving flags and cheering loudly. It was a moving and inspiring moment for Dominique. When she and her teammates reached the bars, they quickly set down their bags, kicked off their blue flip-flops, and walked up the podium steps to greet the judges. They stood in order of height in front of the officials and listened to a word of encouragement. It was customary in gymnastics for teams to present themselves to the judges before each event. The head judge usually said something like "Good luck, ladies" then dismissed the group to warm up.

The meet began, and Jaycie and Kerri got the team off to a great start. Dominique went third. She flew from bar to bar with enormous, breathtaking release moves and capped off her well-designed routine with a full-twisting double layout. She stuck the landing, but her arms wavered a little—her only noticeable error.

"Yes, yes, yes!" Bela cried while pumping his fist. In the stands, Dimitry and Camelia embraced delightedly.

After hugging Marta and Jaycie, Dominique made her way over to Bela, who was again behind the barrier. He reached over and gave her a congratulatory hug then reminded her to get ready for beam. He did not want Dominique to dwell on her bar routine. She needed to be thinking about her next event.

Dominique quickly stashed her grips in the little blue bag USA Gymnastics had given her when she first made the national team four years prior. Though it was faded and worn, she still carried it around, believing it brought her good luck. She also had seven guardian angel pins fastened to the bag that watched over her at meets.

Amy, Shannon, and the other Dominique continued the momentum on bars with impressive sets that put the U.S. in the lead for the first time in Olympic history.

The Americans remained indomitable on beam. Amanda and Jaycie got the ball rolling. Kerri, Dominique Dawes, and Shannon brought in the big scores, leaving Dominique as the anchor. She confidently mounted and spryly danced down the beam. She was exquisite. She did not hesitate. She did not wobble.

When she stuck her dismount, Bela lifted his arms and eyes to the heavens and clapped his hands in jubilation. He turned to hug any American coach he could find.

"We've done it!" he shouted.

Dominique briefly embraced each teammate as she made her way to Bela. "That's what we're talking about," he said excitedly. He kissed her cheek. "Good job, little piggy!"

The U.S. women were pulling for one another more than they had in past meets. While not as unified as some of the other teams who trained together year round, the coaches and athletes were hugging and congratulating each other. Such displays had been absent from previous competitions.

"This team is more of a family," Dominique Dawes pointed out. "We're all living together in this house, so we see each other a lot more and we're all working together."

On floor, Jaycie and Amanda got the crowd going with personable exercises. Dominique followed and worked the audience into a frenzy with her energized *"Devil Went Down to Georgia"* routine. As her teammates had done, she nailed all of her tumbling passes and made the set look effortless. The crowd thundered approvingly as she finished and jogged off the mat.

Dominique Dawes, Shannon, and Kerri further widened the gap between the U.S. and the Russians. As the Americans marched to vault, they held a firm grip on first place. It looked like victory would be theirs. All they had to do was hit their vaults—for that matter, only *one* vault each, because the best of the two counted.

Jaycie started off solidly, fidgeting only slightly on the landing. Amy and Shannon played it conservatively by doing an easier vault first. With an adequate score in the bank, each threw a difficult vault on the second attempt. The strategy was sound, except neither could stick the landing. Dominique Dawes also vaulted well but hopped slightly at the end. The team's scores were good, but not great.

Dominique walked up the steps to the podium knowing she could win it all for the Americans. If she hit her vaults, the gold was theirs. The Russians were doing well on floor, and since vault finished ahead of floor, Dominique did not know exactly what score she needed. But the U.S. enjoyed a sizable lead, so a solid vault would surely be enough.

When given the signal, Dominique bolted down the runway—arms pumping, jaw clenched. She hammered the board and flew back to the horse. Her hands made contact. She pushed off. She flipped. After one-and-a-half twists, her arms jetted to the side in preparation for landing. She opened up—too soon—and her feet struck the mat. But her rotation had been cut short, and she could not help but sit down.

Surprised, Dominique quickly stood and acknowledged the judges. "I was so upset, like, 'Wait a second. This doesn't happen to me,' " she later recalled. "But I knew only the best vault counts, so I still had a chance."

As she walked back up the runway, she glanced over at Bela, who naturally had suggestions for improvement. Her face now registered concern. The carefree smile was gone, in its place a serious, worried expression. Dominique's heart was pounding as she found her starting marker, seventy-eight feet from the vault. "Come on," she told herself. "Fight. Stick." She had done this vault countless times. Sure, she had not practiced it as much recently, but she knew how to do it. Besides wanting to clinch the gold for her team, she needed a good score to make it into the all-around final. Only the top three Americans would qualify.

The green light glowed, and she turned her gaze toward the judges but did not see them. Her mind was racing. She raised her arms over her head and quickly dropped them to her side. This was not her usual salute. It expressed no confidence. It showed no spark. No glimpse of a smile—just an intense stare. It was not the salute she had practiced hundreds of times in front of Bela and Marta so it would be just right. She was going through the motions as though on autopilot, allowing her mind a few more precious seconds to replay the vault correctly and impress the movements upon her willing limbs.

Determination blazed in her eyes as she stepped forward. As before, she raced down the runway. Again, she struck the board firmly and pushed off the padded horse. Again, she flipped and twisted through the air.

Again, she landed with a thud and sat down.

The crowd gasped in disbelief. Bela turned his head and covered his eyes as though wincing from a painful blow to the face.

"I can't believe it," he muttered over and over.

Stunned, Dominique jogged over to Marta. She could not believe she had missed both vaults. She did not look at her teammates as she walked past them, feeling she had let them down along with her parents, her coaches, and herself. She busied herself with putting her shoes into her bag, refusing to even take a peek at the 9.20 on the scoreboard.

"I knew I could do the vault," Dominique said later, wiping away a tear. "Just at the last minute, I couldn't make it around."

"She hasn't vaulted for a long, long time," Bela reasoned. "Ever since [Nationals] she hasn't done any kind of landing on the hard surfaces."

Kerri, the final vaulter, stepped up to bat needing at least a 9.493 to seal the victory. With that score, the Russians would not be able to surpass the U.S. no matter what their final two athletes did on floor.

On her first try, Kerri buckled under the pressure and sat down like her teammate had done moments earlier. The spirited crowd became suddenly subdued. The gold, which had seemed so solidly within their grasp, was no longer a lock. Kerri, who had often found herself training in the shadow of another star, was now center stage. Not Kim Zmeskal. Not Shannon Miller. Not Dominique Moceanu. The world was watching her.

But no one knew how serious Kerri's predicament really was. Upon landing, she had heard a pop from her ankle. When she stood up, severe pain shot through her left foot. She gingerly walked back to her starting marker, shaking her foot and trying not to limp.

She looked to Bela. "Shake it out," he barked. "You can do it. You can do it. *You can do it!*"

She had hurt her ankles before. Sometimes they hurt badly for a few seconds, then the pain subsided. She hoped that would be the case this time, but in the back of her mind she knew it would not. Everything was happening so fast. She was by herself on the podium and did not have time to explain how badly she was hurt. A 9.162 flashed on the scoreboard.

On the sidelines, Dominique had mixed feelings. She wanted Kerri to do well so the team would win, but she desperately wanted to make the all-around final. Nonetheless, she joined her teammates and the fans in spurring Kerri on.

Kerri had the weight of the world—or at least a nation—on her small shoulders. She kept telling herself not to fall or all the years of hard work and effort would be squandered in a few seconds and the gold would slip away. She had dealt with excruciating pain before. Surely she could endure it long enough to do this one last vault.

"Please, God, help me out," she prayed silently. "Let me do this vault one more time. I've done it thousands and thousands of times. Let me do it one more time."

Kerri raised her arms to the judges, and a hush fell over the spectators. She bolted forward and her feet pounded down the narrow blue runway. Whack! She hit the springboard and her hands pushed off the vault. She launched herself through the air as 32,620 fans simultaneously held their breaths.

In a brief moment that came to epitomize the 1996 Olympic Games like no other, Kerri pulled out the vault of her life.

The roof was nearly blown off the Georgia Dome as the American fans erupted in a collective shout of triumph. The U.S. had won the gold medal for the first time in history! But something about the scene did not look quite right. Oddly, Kerri finished the vault holding her left foot in the air, and she turned to acknowledge the judges by hopping on one leg. The deafening roar quickly subsided when Kerri's face contorted in pain and she collapsed, crawling on all fours off the mat.

Marta was quickly at her side. "I can't walk!" Kerri cried to her coach. "Please help me!" Marta and trainer Barb Pearson helped her off the podium, and she was carried to a nearby stretcher. Not wanting to miss what was perhaps *the* photo opportunity of the Games, television cameras and photographers surrounded her.

Racked with pain, Kerri hardly noticed the thunderous applause brought on by the posting of her score, a 9.712. The score clinched the victory for the United States. It also knocked Dominique to fourth place on the U.S. team, disqualifying her for the all-around competition. The rest of the team, still in shock and afraid to believe they had really won, did not know if they should celebrate or worry about their fallen teammate.

"Is she okay?" Shannon asked Dominique.

"I don't know," Dominique responded with concern, trying to see where Kerri had been taken.

"What did she do?"

"I don't know what she did on the first vault," Dominique mumbled irritably, giving Shannon a look that seemed to say "How should I know?" as she walked away in mid-sentence.

Over near the floor, the Russians cried openly, unable to conceal their disappointment. The final Russian competitor, Roza Galieva, had earned only a 9.50 on floor. She wept bitterly, blaming her low score on the crowd noise that had left her unable to hear her floor music. The Romanians were equally dejected and sat by the bars looking stunned. They had been favored to win but had only placed third. The Russians, at least, could be proud to have clinched the silver even after finishing fourth at the 1995 World Championships.

As it turned out, Kerri's second vault had not been the deciding factor. Because of the United States' considerable lead going into the last event and the adequate scores of the first five vaulters, Dominique's 9.20 on vault had been enough to win the gold. However, at the time no one could have predicted how well the last two Russians would do on floor.

The U.S. women marched back to the warmup gym and waited for the awards ceremony to begin. Kerri, who had been taken backstage for some quick medical attention, was adamant about standing on the podium and receiving her gold medal. However, the doctors feared her leg was broken and insisted she go immediately to the hospital. In desperation, Kerri summoned Bela for help.

"No way," he told the doctors. "This girl just helped our team win the gold medal. This is the first time the USA women's gymnastics team has accomplished this feat, so if I have to stop the police, I'm letting her go on that medal stand."

Bela prevailed because, as Kerri later put it, "Everyone listens to Bela." Several minutes later, she was wheeled out and encircled by her teammates and coaches. Bela gently lifted her from the stretcher and carried her into the arena.

The applause was deafening as the U.S. team marched onto the floor podium smiling and waving. On cue, they stepped onto the awards stand when the announcer proclaimed them the gold medalists. Together, Dominique and Shannon helped their injured teammate up the steps. The frenzied crowd began chanting "U-S-A! U-S-A!" as, one by one, the seven women received their hard-won gold. When it was her turn, Dominique leaned forward so the shiny medal could be draped around her neck. She shook the presenter's hand and accepted a bouquet of flowers. After each had received her award, the champions lifted their flowers and smiled before a sea of camera flashes that sparkled across the arena like a thousand fireflies on a summer night.

Bela and Marta had waited a lifetime to see one of their teams defeat the Russians in an Olympic competition. This was the first time the Russian women had ever lost.

Bela turned to his wife of thirty-three years and stated simply, "We did it." Marta shook her head in amazement. Bela gently kissed her forehead and said with bittersweet finality, "The last time."

"The last time," Marta repeated. "Fantastic! A gold!"

"Twenty years ago a big one, and now a big one," Bela mused.

Theirs had been a career marked by champions. "1976, Nadia was like a first love," Bela later remarked. "I was a young coach, and that was a tremendous victory. It was a beautiful page on my professional career. 1984 was *strong*. Mary Lou, the first American all-around Olympic Champion, standing behind her and helping her was again an unforgettable experience. But tonight, I had something even more intense. I felt the joy, the pride, and the victory from seven young athletes."

The boisterous arena quieted as the announcer's voice boomed, "Would you please rise for the national anthem of the United States of America." Dominique placed her hand over her heart as the first chords of *"The Star-Spangled Banner"* began. She sang along and stared at the flag as it slowly rose before her.

It was beautiful to behold: the U.S. team, adorned with gold medals and flower bouquets, standing together on the podium and singing proudly to their flag and to their country. What a glorious day for America!

"It was a great feeling," Dominique said afterwards. "This moment will be cherished forever."

The anthem ended, and the team huddled together one last time to share this moment of victory. They talked about how far they had come as a team and what a good job they had done. Again, Dominique and Shannon helped Kerri off the stand and into the arms of Bela, who carried her back to the stretcher while the rest of the team took a victory lap around the arena.

The group—minus Kerri—was ushered to a press room to answer questions. "We cheered for each other," Dominique told reporters. "We just kept going, and we were a really great team tonight." Still, she admitted she had mixed feelings about the evening. Winning the gold medal was tremendously exciting, yet

159

it was very disappointing not to make the all-around. "Kerri showed how strong a gymnast can be," she acknowledged. But if she were needed to take Kerri's slot in the all-around, she made her feelings clear: "It would be great for me."

When an athlete who had qualified to the all-around final became injured, her country substituted another person in her place. Dominique was the next highest finisher—fourth on the U.S. team and eleventh overall—so she was the alternate. To qualify to the all-around final, a gymnast had to place in the top thirty-six during the team competition subject to a three-per-country limitation. The top three U.S. finishers had been Shannon, Dominique Dawes, and Kerri.

For now, it did not matter who would compete in the all-around. Tonight, they were celebrities, every one of them, and to make it official they were invited to the Planet Hollywood restaurant for a party given in their honor by movie stars Bruce Willis and Demi Moore.

Kerri was still missing. At a local hospital she had been diagnosed with a severe sprain and a few torn ligaments. The news was not encouraging, but at least nothing was broken.

Kerri had her own press conference after her trip to the hospital. Many questioned whether she should have done the second vault since it was later discovered the team did not need it to win.

"A lot of people are criticizing Bela for encouraging me to do it," she responded, "but I'm eighteen. I'm an adult. I make my own choices. It was definitely my decision and kind of a matter of pride. I didn't want to be remembered for falling on my butt in my best event."

Part way through her press conference, Kerri received word that the rest of the team was at Planet Hollywood and she was welcome to join them.

Security guards had to hold back the exuberant fans outside Planet Hollywood from closing in on the "Magnificent Seven," as the team came to be known. Once inside, everyone wondered what the team would eat. Cheeseburgers, french fries, and milk shakes were not exactly healthy and low in fat.

"This is once in a lifetime, so it doesn't matter," Bela laughed. However, the gymnasts did enjoy specially-prepared meals.

"We had some spaghetti," Dominique said. "[I had] a virgin strawberry daiquiri. All of us did."

After eating and picking up some free souvenirs like Planet Hollywood jean jackets, it was time for more fun. Bruce got the crowd going with the familiar "U-S-A" chant. Just as he began apologizing that Kerri could not make it, she hobbled in on crutches. The crowd cheered, and Kerri thanked everyone for making her feel so special.

As exciting as it was for the team to meet Bruce and Demi, the Hollywood couple claimed it was equally thrilling for them to meet the team. "Their focus and determination is to be commended," Demi said.

"And how about the drama?" Bruce jumped in. "The girl sprains her ankle and saves the day with that last vault. It was just great! It was just really cool!"

"It wouldn't have been believable as a movie," Demi joked.

Even the President of the United States had been captivated by the intense drama. He and ninety-nine million Americans had tuned in by television. "I was in California," Bill Clinton explained. "We watched [NBC's] reporting of the gymnastics competition through one of the four events, then I had to go to two different meetings. Then I came out and got on the plane. I asked one person to tape it and I said, 'If you tell me or anybody else what happened, I'll just cream ya.' So we had the whole airplane biting our fingernails as if we were watching it live. And it must have been three or four o'clock in the morning [Eastern] time when we finally saw the fabulous ending of it."

Once back at Connally House, or "Tara" as the team called it, Dominique still could not believe she had won the gold. The medal was heavier than it looked. Although not pure gold, it was made of sterling silver topped with six grams of gold.

The next morning, Dominique awoke early after only a few hours of sleep. Already, the house was bustling with activity. Flowers with notes of congratulation were pouring in, and the *Today* show was setting up for an interview with the team.

The gymnasts dressed in matching red sweaters and white skirts. Katie Couric interviewed them. Not surprisingly, she asked Dominique what had happened on her vault.

"I guess I just lost focus and wasn't concentrating enough on what I had to do," Dominique answered hoarsely. "I guess I just got too excited. . . . It was a mistake, but I'm really glad the team did really well."

Later the group was on CBS's *This Morning*, and other interviews continued throughout the day. Everyone was wondering whether Kerri would compete in the all-around.

"It's too early to say," she maintained. "I'm really going to try. This is the Olympics, what I tried so long and hard for."

For all Kerri's bravery, Dominique knew there was a good chance she would compete in Kerri's place. "If it comes to that, I'll be ready," she declared. "I really hope Kerri gets better because she is my teammate and we are friends. I hope her foot gets better soon because I know she's worked hard for this moment."

"We're going to have a workout in the afternoon, so we will know much more tonight," Bela said.

All Dominique could do was wait and wonder.

Chapter 10

Fame and Fortune

"Tonight we made a decision," Bela announced Wednesday about Kerri's competitive status. "She has to be out. The leg is badly swollen and she is hurting. But there is still an opportunity to see her back four days from now in the event finals."

It was official. Dominique would compete in the all-around in Kerri's place. In a way, she would be competing for both of them.

"That's the responsibility Dominique is going to have to carry with her," Bela suggested. "And she knows this."

On the Romanian team, another gymnast found herself in a situation exactly opposite that of Dominique. Alexandra Marinescu, who had qualified for the all-around final, was pulled out by her coach Octavian Belu and replaced by Simona Amanar. Unlike the Soviets had done in years past, Octavian did not invent an injury to explain the replacement. He merely stated that Alexandra had not been working hard enough. However, since she was the only team member to have come from a different gymnastics club in Romania, some speculated the decision had been politically motivated. Octavian would no longer have to answer to his government because he was leaving Romania for the United States.

Gymnastics fans were disappointed that Dominique would not be pitted against Alexandra at these Games. About the same age and size, the two had been considered rivals ever since Alexandra's arrogant comments about Dominique at a November 1995 meet: "I don't have any emotions regarding her. I have competed against girls who are much better than her."[1] She had also told Nadia Comaneci in an interview that Dominique "has a lot of things to learn." Despite such talk, Dominique had defeated Alexandra in all their pre-Olympic confrontations.

On Thursday, July 25, Dominique awoke to the realization that today's meet was the most important one of her life. Her naturally competitive nature kicked into overdrive as she remembered how it had felt to win the 1995 U.S. Championships. She longed to be atop the awards stand again.

"The best part is knowing you are winning," she remarked, brown eyes gleaming. "That last moment in the last event, when you stick it, and you just *know* it! And everybody's cheering. It's a good feeling standing up there."[2]

To medal, Dominique had to hit every routine without any breaks. She did not perform the most difficult skills on each event, so to earn the big scores she would have to give the judges no reason to take deductions.

Bela ruled out having Dominique use her new beam and floor

skills since she had not practiced them enough recently. He typically played it conservatively in big meets. His gymnasts did not throw the most risky tricks, but they were usually solid competitors with clean routines.

After a brilliant coaching career spanning six Olympic Games, Bela was in all likelihood participating in his last. "We all knew pretty much this would be it for him," Dominique said sadly. "Definitely, it makes making this team a lot more special. I want to close it out for him with a good ending. I want to show him how much he's done for me and how much I love him."

Dominique had been preparing for more than a decade for the evening's competition, and she was ready. "I just have to do my routines one more time," she thought to herself. "I've done them a million times in practice, and just one more time I have to do them really well."

Bela informed Dominique that she would be starting on beam and would be the first one up. She frowned. Starting on beam did not make for a good competition order, and going first only made it worse. She pushed the bad news out of her mind and concentrated on her warmup.

When the general warmup in the practice gym ended, the athletes were notified that the meet would be delayed twenty minutes. Since they were not allowed back on the equipment, everyone kept warm and loose by practicing skills on the floor mat.

The delay had been caused by extra security measures for the President, who was in attendance. Spectators were a little annoyed at having to wait outside in the heat for nearly an hour, their progress hindered by two crowd-control checkpoints and a very thorough Presidential security check in addition to the usual Olympic security screening. Some were delayed beyond the start of the meet. When the reason for the delay was announced, many in the audience booed. The President later received more boos when he was pictured on the large screen in the arena.

When the meet finally began, Dominique marched over to beam and began the touch warmup. The athletes warmed up in the order in which they would compete. As the others took their turn, she waited nervously on the podium, tugging on her leotard, making sure everything was in place, telling herself she could do it.

Soon Dominique stood alone on the podium. It was time to begin. When given the green light, she raised and lowered her arms, hopped on the springboard, and flipped upside down into her shoulder roll. She smoothly twisted down the beam then stood and danced to one end. She nailed her three layouts without so much as a quiver and aggressively executed her leaps. Everything was going as planned.

Dominique took two steps, punched the beam, and flipped forward. As she landed, her shoulder dipped to the right and her body leaned precariously. Her right leg shot up and her arms flailed about as she desperately attempted to regain her balance. She managed to stay on, but the wobble would result in a significant deduction. She calmly finished the remainder of the set and stuck the dismount.

Dominique's expressionless stare could not hide her disappointment as she approached Marta, who welcomed her with open arms. "It could be stronger," Marta gently chided, "but that's all right." Marta continued going over the routine as Dominique took off her beam shoes.

A 9.60 was flashed on the scoreboard. She knew the score would most likely drop her out of gold medal contention. When the first rotation ended, she was in seventeenth place.

On her second event, Dominique shook her legs to stay loose while she waited for the previous gymnast's score. Bela was relatively passive on the sidelines—not a good sign. Dominique started her floor set with a smile, but it vanished when she stepped out of bounds on her first tumbling pass. Nonetheless, she kept her chin up and playfully danced through the rest of the routine. Her other three tumbling runs were flawless. After holding her ending pose for a few seconds, she turned to acknowledge the judges then jogged off the mat.

"Good job," Bela said without his usual enthusiasm while giving her a quick hug. He knew that small step over the white line had knocked her out of the running. Bela sat down, a rare sight at a competition, and continued, "The rest of it was good. The dance was nice and your face was happy."

Dominique scored a 9.687, which moved her up only two places to fifteenth. Her teammates Dominique Dawes and Shannon were one and two, respectively, going into the third rotation. Unfortunately, both had mistakes on floor that dropped them out of medal contention as well. It was not looking good for the United States.

Dominique was on vault, her nemesis from the team final, in the third round. She was determined to stand up both vaults and redeem herself. On her first attempt, she landed on her feet but took a big hop forward. She pulled out all the stops on her second try and stuck it cold. Her face broke into a broad smile, and she ran over to Bela.

"That's what you're supposed to do!" he exclaimed, engulfing her in a warm bear hug. "All right, little piggy, good job."

The average of both vaults was a 9.706, a score that did not sit well with the crowd and earned the judges a few boos. With nothing to lose on her final event, Dominique was aggressive. She took each release move to the limit. However, she piked down her full-twisting double layout dismount, which caused a hop on the landing. She walked over to Bela and received a quick embrace, but she did not say anything. Showing no emotion, she found her bag and slowly put her grips away. She scored a 9.762 and finished ninth.

Several gymnasts—Svetlana Khorkina, Dina Kochetkova, and Mo Huilan—had significant errors in the last round, making it easy for Ukraine's Lilia Podkopayeva to step in and win the meet. Gina Gogean clinched second, and her teammates Simona Amanar and Lavinia Milosovici tied for third.

Lilia admitted it was gratifying to beat the Americans since she had experienced such a lukewarm reception from the American audience. The crowd noise had been disturbing, especially on floor. Eventually she had gotten used to it, but it had left a sour taste in her mouth.

Such criticism was not entirely fair. Although the largely-American audience had been naturally biased in favor of its own team, the fans certainly had not heckled or otherwise mistreated any foreign gymnasts. The applause had been light for some of their routines, but without an announcer it had been hard for many to tell which ones were the foreign stars. Besides, with all events going simultaneously like a four-ring circus, most viewers had been able to concentrate on only one event at a time—usually one on which an athlete from their own country was competing.

Such was the advantage of playing at home. "You cannot take away the patriotic feeling of the country that has the opportunity to cheer for their own athletes," Bela stated. "It's never been done and it never will be done. It's part of sports."

But being crowd favorites had disadvantages as well. Enormous pressure and high expectations were heaped on the hometown athletes.

Even after a lackluster performance, the media came rushing at Dominique to get her reaction. "It's disappointing because you want to be up there with everybody else," a watery-eyed Dominique confessed. "This is only the second big international meet that I've ever been to. I'm the youngest one competing and I've accomplished a lot. It's the Olympics and I still got a gold medal. I can look at that and remember. I might have some goals after this to keep continuing, or—we'll see. I'm not sure yet."

When NBC commentator Beth Ruyak asked if she wanted to "yell and cry and jump and scream in a room somewhere and then start all over again," Dominique responded, "I might. I feel like that, but we'll see."

Following the competition, the U.S. team was invited to meet the President, the First Lady, and their daughter Chelsea. The gymnasts had a few souvenir photographs taken with the Clintons.

Two days after the all-around final, a tragedy devastated Atlanta and shocked the entire world. Early in the morning on July 27, a bomb exploded next to a speaker tower in the Olympic Park, killing two people and injuring over one hundred others. After learning about the blast, the U.S. women's gymnastics coaches were thankful they had taken so many precautions to safeguard their athletes.

"Everyone was talking about our secret training site and our secret house, but now those same people are probably asking why they didn't do the same," Steve Nunno remarked.

Dominique and her teammates were in the middle of a much-needed break from competition when the incident occurred. The coaches tried to shelter the team from the commotion and round-the-clock media coverage of the bombing so they would not lose their focus on the competition ahead.

Despite the cowardly act of terrorism, the Games continued. Monday was the final day of gymnastics competition. Dominique had qualified to two event finals, beam and floor, and she was really hoping to medal on one of them. Beam was probably her best chance.

Again, Dominique was disappointed with her draw on beam—second. Following a disastrous routine by Alexandra Marinescu, Dominique stepped onto the podium and was greeted by loud cheers. The judges were deciding Alexandra's score, so Dominique had to stand and wait in front of the capacity crowd. This was nerve-wracking. It was easy to get cold and distracted.

"Calm," Bela called to her from the sidelines.

Eventually, Alexandra's 8.462 was announced, and Dominique was allowed to begin. She mounted cleanly, danced to the end of the beam, then raised her arms over her head and began a four-trick tumbling sequence. Her back handspring was square, as was her first layout. However, on her second layout her foot skidded out from under her and down the beam as if it were greased. Unable to stop the sequence in mid-air, she arched back and tried to pull around her third layout. It was not high enough, and her head crashed into the beam. Instinctively, she grabbed the bottom of the apparatus with her hands and wrapped herself around it. She finished the maneuver sitting on the beam and striking an impromptu pose.

The fall would result in a huge deduction, and Dominique knew it. Another of her medal hopes had been dashed. But the unwritten code of conduct honored by all gymnasts demanded that she never give up. Though it seemed hopeless, she could not quit. She had to finish her routine.

Abiding by the code she had learned from her coaches, her teammates, her rivals, and her idols, she stood and continued as though nothing had happened.

The rest of the routine was solid. She even stuck her dismount. But she was shaken and frustrated as she walked over to Marta. Her head hurt—a lump was forming—but the pain of defeat was much worse. She scored a dismal 9.125. While Dominique sat wondering why she seemed to have such bad luck in the event finals, Shannon performed the best beam routine of her life to win the gold in what was possibly her final Olympic appearance.

Dominique's last event of the Olympics was the floor exercise. She was up sixth and determined to finish on a good note. The routine sparkled. Her difficulty was not the highest, but her personality shone the brightest. She drew the audience into the set with her dazzling smile and lively music and even hit her new pass, two consecutive full-twisting front flips.

Bela gave Dominique a "good job" and a hug. She had done an excellent routine that was worth a 9.825 and, for the moment, third place. But Lilia and Mo were still to come. Although Mo had a few stumbles that knocked her out of contention, Lilia surpassed everyone with her balletic style to win the gold. Dominique had to settle for fourth and no individual medal at the Games.

The Olympics had not been everything she had hoped. She was pleased with the team gold medal, but she knew she had been capable of earning an individual one as well. She might have felt differently if she had done her best and still come up short, but she knew in her heart that she could have done better on several events.

Dominique put these unsettling thoughts aside and tried to seem cheery, despite only a few hours of sleep, for the team's Tuesday appearance on *Good Morning America*. Fortunately, interviewer Donna deVarona did not ask her any questions about her mediocre showing.

In the afternoon, the team participated in the Champions Gala. For the show, Dominique, Amanda, and Jaycie simultaneously performed parts of the compulsory beam set as a tribute to the compulsories, which would no longer be done at the elite level. In the finale, the U.S. team performed a stirring group exercise. One by one they danced out on the mat to the inspiring instrumental *"On American Shores"* by John Tesh, who was honored they had chosen his music. Together, the women performed a dance segment from the compulsory floor routine as *"Georgia"* echoed sentimentally throughout the arena. Switching gears, they got the crowd going with *"YMCA"* and *"Macarena"* as they did the obligatory hand motions and danced playfully around the floor. They finished their upbeat presentation to the patriotic song *"God Bless the USA."* The crowd went wild, snapping pictures and screaming for their heroes.

The gold-medal-winning Russian men's team rushed out onto the floor bearing flowers for each American gymnast. Russian heartthrob Alexei Nemov handed Dominique her bouquet and kissed her on both cheeks. Then he lifted her high in the air. She was a little surprised, but she smiled and waved to the crowd. The two teams went to the edge of the mat to wave to the fans, and Alexei could not resist kissing Dominique's cheek one more time. She glanced back at him then turned to run off the mat with the others.

Now that all the Olympic gymnastics was finally over, it was time for Dominique to have some fun. She took in some shopping at the Athlete's Village. One of her hobbies was collecting souvenir spoons from all the many cities to which she traveled. She also went to a basketball game and saw the Dream Team play.

Outside of winning a gold medal, the biggest thrill of the Games was actually getting to meet the Dream Team. An informal meeting of the two teams was set up after Kerri mentioned her one wish was to meet Hakeem Olajuwon. Since many on the

Dream Team were just as anxious to meet the gymnasts, nearly the entire squad showed up. Dominique was so excited she boldly ran up to Hakeem and suggested the two take a photograph together. She barely came up to his hip.

"How tall are you?" she questioned.

"Six-foot eleven," he replied. "How tall are you?"

"Four-foot six."

"Oh my."

Dominique met NBA legends Scottie Pippen, Reggie Miller, Penny Hardaway, Karl Malone, Gary Payton, and David Robinson, who showed off by executing a few handstands. Shaquille O'Neal even lifted Dominique off the floor to give her a big hug.

"Now I do feel like a giant," he exclaimed. "Of course, you know I taught them all they know: the flips, the tumbles, the horse, everything."

After trading stories, pins, and souvenirs with everyone but Charles Barkley, the gymnasts prepared to leave. They took the elevator to the lobby, and when the doors opened, there was Sir Charles himself.

"You didn't think you were getting away without seeing me, did you?"[3] he asked.

The Magnificent Seven were very popular everywhere they went. On Sunday, the final day of the Olympics, it was announced at a press conference that the group would be featured on one of five Olympic Wheaties cereal boxes. Before the Olympics, executives at General Mills, the maker of Wheaties, had talked about putting Dominique by herself on a box if she won an individual gold medal. However, after the spectacular team competition, General Mills decided to feature the entire team on the package.

Dominique's busy schedule continued beyond the Olympics. She flew to New York City for an appearance with most of her teammates on the *Late Show with David Letterman*, then she went to Washington, D.C., to attend a party for all the American Olympians hosted by the President at the White House. When she finally returned to Houston, Dominique was greeted by many fans at the Intercontinental Airport. She signed some autographs, then her parents escorted her to a limousine waiting to take her home. As she walked into her house for the first time in a month, all she could see were piles of fan mail, stuffed animals, flowers, and assorted gifts. Some of the packages were simply addressed "Dominique Moceanu, Houston, Texas" or "Dominique Moceanu, Karolyi's Gymnastics." She wondered how they had even reached her. In addition to her home and gym addresses, she had a special fan club address where she received mail. Budding young gymnasts wrote to tell her how much she inspired them. Some mentioned how they wanted to become gymnasts just like her.

Dominique and her mom plowed through as much mail as they could. Since it was impossible to personalize each response, Dominique decided to send out a photocopy of a handwritten letter to her fans.

"Thank you so much for your letters, gifts, and wonderful support," she wrote. "Your response has been absolutely overwhelming! As much as I would like to answer each and every letter personally, my time and schedule will not permit me to. Winning the team gold medal at the Olympics was a lifelong dream come true, and I'm proud to be a member of the first women's team to win a gold medal. We will be on tour very soon, so hopefully I'll see you in your town!"

The Olympics had changed her life. People began noticing her more than ever, even when she was in street clothes and she wore her hair down. Enrollment in gymnastics clubs all over the country swelled because of her team's accomplishment.

The magnitude of one summer night's competition was finally starting to sink in. "It's going to remain in the history books forever," Dominique said in amazement. "All of our names are going to be there forever. And we all did it together."

Dominique had always thought she would retire following the 1996 Games. But she had not done as well as she had hoped, which gave her a reason to keep going until the 2000 Olympics. She would only be eighteen then, a year younger than Shannon and Dominique Dawes had been at the 1996 Games.

"I won't be too old," Dominique allowed, "but you don't know how your body will hold up. You have to go through all that changing and stuff."[4]

"Personally, I hope she doesn't retire," said Kim Zmeskal. "I've had five or six really close teammates, and for the most part all of us regret thinking that you're supposed to retire once you try for one Olympics."

Even gold-medalist sprinter Michael Johnson thought Dominique should continue. While giving her an autograph at the Games, he had encouraged her to try again in four years because she was so young.

Still, the thought of lounging at home after school and doing the things other teenagers did was appealing. She could watch her favorite television programs—*Friends*, *The Fresh Prince of Bel-Air*, and *Ricki Lake*—without having to program the VCR. She could hang out at the Galleria mall and shop more frequently at her favorite stores: *Gap for Kids*, *Limited Too*, and *The Disney Store*. She could go to more sporting events, like Houston Rockets basketball games, of which she was a big fan. She could watch her favorite movie stars, Brad Pitt and Jim Carrey, more often on the big screen. Or better yet, she could indulge in white-chocolate-mousse frozen yogurt without feeling guilty.

175

For now, her decision would have to wait. She went back to the gym to prepare for some professional meets and the post-Olympic tour. Naturally, she experienced a bit of a letdown after just competing in the meet for which she had been training her whole life. It was hard to get excited about practicing again, especially when she thought about the four long years until the next Olympics.

Besides going back to the gym, in mid-August she re-enrolled at Northland Christian School. Thankfully, her intensive training schedule and education via videotape had not set her back. In fact, her September birthday made her one of the youngest students in the sophomore class. Some of her classmates were learning to drive, but because of her age she would have to wait another year before getting behind the wheel.

Dominique was happy to be back with her old friends. The school even proclaimed Saturday, August 24 as "Dominique Day." She was honored during a volleyball tournament and given a school letter jacket. She also signed some autographs for the crowd that had shown up to celebrate her Olympic accomplishments.

On Labor Day, Dominique participated in a meet at the Summit in Houston billed as "U.S. Versus the World: The Ultimate Gymnastics Competition." This professional meet pitted members of the gold-medal-winning team against a group of the world's best female gymnasts. The Americans had a slight advantage since it was their entire squad—minus Kerri—against Roza Galieva, Svetlana Khorkina, Svetlana Boginskaya, Mo Huilan, Bi Wenjing of China, and Yvonne Tousek of Canada.

Dominique began on floor. Because her leg was still bothering her, she watered down her tumbling. But her dance was fantastic, and the hometown fans loved it. She received the loudest applause of anyone, and the judges awarded her a 9.90.

On her next event, bars, she was magnificent. She easily hit her two release moves, a Shaposhnikova and a Gienger, and stuck her double layout dismount. When she earned only a 9.725, the biased crowd voiced their displeasure with loud boos.

On beam, her last event, Dominique was smooth and confident. After a dismount accentuated by an exuberant bounce, she smiled and waved to the crowd then exited the podium. Her teammates congratulated her for a job well done. She received a 9.90 to secure the victory for the United States.

"It was a lot of fun," Dominique said afterwards. "All my friends from school are here."

While at the Summit, the U.S. entourage did some exploring. Dominique, Shannon, Amanda, and Jaycie found their way into the Houston Rockets' locker room. Dominique tried on Hakeem Olajuwon's jersey for fun.

"Nice dress," she observed as the bottom of the shirt scraped her shoes.

Two weeks later, Dominique entered the Professional World Team Championships held at Riverfront Coliseum in Cincinnati. This two-day event featured four teams: two from the United States, one from China, and one from Russia. Each team consisted of two men and three women. Dominique was on the USA-1 squad with Shannon, Amy, John Macready, and Chainey Umphrey.

In the preliminaries, the men went first, putting the team in second place. Three hours later the women began. Interestingly, Bela was on hand but did not coach Dominique. Instead, Artur Akopyan did the spotting and instruction. Dominique was aggressive on bars and beam, and she wowed the crowd on floor. The meet concluded at midnight with Dominique and her teammates trailing USA-2 by less than a tenth.

The finals were held the next day. This time the men and

women performed together on three events each. Dominique was strong on bars and solid on beam, scoring 9.85s on both. Unfortunately, Chainey suffered a scary fall on his second event, high bar, that so disoriented him he withdrew from the competition. However, the team was not disqualified since the lowest score in each round was dropped.

Dominique was the last person to compete in the final round. She needed a good performance to move her team ahead of the other U.S. group. Her vibrant floor set was more than adequate, earning a lofty 9.975.

"After it was over, my teammates Shannon and Amy were telling me all I needed was like a 9.80," Dominique said. "I was surprised. We did it. It was a good team effort. We all did really well tonight."

Following the Professional Worlds, Dominique began the thirty-four-city John Hancock Tour of World Gymnastics Champions. Since she would be missing the first several months of tenth grade, she brought along a tutor to help her keep up with her studies. During the exhibitions, she performed on floor and beam. She also did a group floor routine with five of her gold-medal-winning teammates.

Kerri was the only member of the Olympic squad not to go on this tour. Instead, she opted for another tour sponsored by Magic Productions and the International Management Group that offered a cool $1 million to each of the Magnificent Seven. Although Dominique and the others had already signed contracts and were obligated to participate in the John Hancock Tour, receiving this other offer still proved beneficial. Originally, they were each to earn $3,500 for every stop on the tour, but after being accused of ripping off the athletes, John Hancock and the tour's other promoters, Bill Graham Presents and Jefferson-Pilot Sports, increased the rate to $5,000 per exhibition.

Dominique's success was proving to be quite lucrative. Along with the other American athletes who had earned gold medals, she received $15,000 from the U.S. Olympic Committee to help offset expenses incurred training for the Games. In addition, she could expect to receive at least $10,000 for each of several made-for-television professional competitions that followed the Olympics. Fees for appearing on a Wheaties box and royalties from a couple book deals, including a children's autobiography entitled <u>Dominique Moceanu: An American Champion</u>, also helped.

While Dominique's earnings were substantial, her father estimated that he had spent at least $200,000 making her an Olympic champion. Dimitry had several different agents for Dominique and was anxious to capitalize on her success. Some suggested that he put too much pressure on his daughter to achieve fame and fortune.

Dominique preferred not to discuss the toll of trying to live up to her father's expectations. "I'm aware of it, yeah," she allowed. "I don't bring it up too much."[5]

With more and more money pouring into the sport, it was not surprising that gymnastics observers began to question the motivation of some athletes. In the past, gymnasts had wanted to become great at their sport because they loved it. Nadia and Mary Lou had not gotten into gymnastics for wealth and fame.

"It's so different now," Bart Conner observed, "because so many of the kids have agents and publicists. The Olympics is big money now. . . . I think a lot of kids, they get involved in the sport for the wrong reason. They get involved because they want to be on the Wheaties box, not because gymnastics is a good thing."

Bart felt that Dominique was motivated by the prospect of becoming a celebrity. "Dominique can really light it up," he said.

"She's adorable, and she knows it. Shannon Miller and some of the other champions, you know they've always wanted to be great *gymnasts*. With Dominique, you know she's always dreamed of being a *star*."[6]

Steve Nunno took it one step further. "Dominique Moceanu is a dynamic personality," he said. "She's very marketable. If she was to get nothing out of gymnastics, then I don't think she'd do it. She's motivated by that."[7]

Dominique loved the sport, but she also didn't mind if it made her famous. "[I'd like] to have them recognize me and not to say, 'Oh, I don't know who she is.' I want them to know who I am and to see I work hard for this. I want them to like me and say, 'Oh, Dominique. I like her.' I want myself to be remembered in history when they talk about gymnastics."

Bela observed, "She wants to be a little star, no doubt about it. She wants to be the best she can be."

Dominique desired the best of both worlds. She planned to continue participating in professional meets, which were typically a lot of fun and not very stressful. She also considered competing in the 1997 World Championships. Not wanting to commit to training until the Sydney Games in 2000, she was just going to take it one meet at a time. Dominique Dawes had said the same thing after the 1992 Olympics and had ended up hanging in there four more years. It was definitely possible for Dominique to do the same. She would have the maturity and experience to be a top contender in 2000.

Epilogue

Dominique has achieved so much already, it is easy to forget how young she is. Scheduled to graduate in 1999, she still has to finish high school. After that, she may pursue a career in sports medicine. For now, gymnastics fills most of her life. Until the flame is lit in Sydney, competing in the next Olympics will remain a possibility for her. If she so chooses, Bela will be there to support her.

"I owe it all to Bela," Dominique once said. "I don't think he will ever understand how much gymnasts like me appreciate him. I hope he never retires again."

"As long as they're going to need me to be around, I'm going to be around them," Bela promised his current gymnasts. "But I won't start another new generation like I have for the past thirty-five years."

Even with all the ups and downs of such a long and colorful coaching career, Bela had nothing but good things to say about his involvement with gymnastics. "I would not regret one second that I spent in gymnastics," he declared. "All the fight and all the frustration and all the low moments, it was worth it. Every and any moment."

Dominique shared his enthusiasm for the sport. "I try looking at it as what I want to make of life, what I want to do," she said. "I want to achieve my goals. That's why I'm doing it. I also love the sport."[1]

From hanging on a clothesline at six months to winning an Olympic gold medal at fourteen, Dominique Moceanu demonstrated a panache and exuberance unmatched by her peers. With the looks of Nadia and the charm of Mary Lou, she reminded the world of past gymnastics greatness while becoming a champion in her own right.

Someday when she looks back on her scrapbook of memories from the first chapters of her life, she will be pleased with what she accomplished. She will benefit from the strong foundation of discipline and determination laid during her years as a gymnast.

Whatever the future holds, Dominique can be proud of a gymnastics career marked by personality and vitality. As a National and Olympic Champion, she will always be remembered as an American gymnastics sensation.

DOMINIQUE MOCEANU

1992 Junior Pan Am Games Winner: Vault, Bars, Floor
1993 Karolyi's Invitational Winner
International Tournament Champion: Beam
1994 Junior National Champion
1995 Reese's Cup Champion: Bars
American Classic Winner: Vault
USA vs. Belarus & China Champion
U.S. Senior National Champion
World Championship Trials Winner
World Silver Medalist: Balance Beam
World Bronze Medalist: Team
Rock-and-Roll Challenge Winner
1996 Reno Challenge Winner: Team
Olympic Gold Medalist: Team
USA vs. the World Winner: Team
Professional World Champion: Team

The youngest American (age 10) to make the U.S. national team.

The youngest American (age 13) to win the U.S. Senior National Championships.

The youngest member (age 14) of the first U.S. women's gymnastics team to win Olympic gold.

GLOSSARY

Double Back: two consecutive back flips; can be done in a tuck, pike, or layout position.

Double Twist: a single layout flip with two twists. Likewise, a triple twist is a single layout flip with three twists.

Flyaway: a bar dismount in which the gymnast swings down from the high bar and lets go to do a flip backwards before landing.

Full-Twisting Double Back: a double back with a full twist on either the first (full-in) or the second (full-out) flip.

Giant Swing: a move in which the gymnast swings all the way around the high bar with a completely outstretched body.

Gienger: a bar release move in which the gymnast does a flyaway with a one-half twist and regrasps the bar. Invented by Eberhard Gienger (Germany).

Layout: a position in which the body is completely outstretched and straight.

Miller: a beam maneuver in which the gymnast does a back dive with a quarter twist to handstand followed by a half pirouette. Invented by Shannon Miller (United States).

Pak Salto: a move in which the gymnast releases the high bar, flips backward, and catches the low bar. Invented by Gyong Sil Pak (North Korea).

Glossary

Pike: a position in which the legs are straight and together with a bend at the waist.

Rudi: a one-and-a-half-twisting front flip.

Shaposhnikova: a free hip circle after which the gymnast lets go of the low bar and grabs the high bar. Invented by Natalia Shaposhnikova (USSR).

Straddle: a position in which the legs are straight but split out to the sides.

Tkatchev (or reverse hecht): a bar release move in which the gymnast swings around the bar, lets go just before reaching a handstand, straddles or pikes his or her legs while flying over the bar, then leans forward to regrasp the bar. Invented by Alexander Tkatchev (USSR).

Tsukahara: a vault in which the gymnast does a half turn onto the vault followed by a back flip. Invented by Mitsuo Tsukahara (Japan).

Tuck: a position in which both knees are bent and brought up to the chest to form a ball with the body.

Whip Back: a back handspring without the hands touching the floor.

Yurchenko: a vault in which a roundoff is done onto the springboard followed by a back handspring onto the vault and a back flip. Invented by Natalia Yurchenko (USSR).

NOTES

Chapter 1 DESTINED FROM BIRTH

1. Mark Starr, "Bounds for Glory," *Newsweek*, October 2, 1995, p. 73.
2. Mark Starr, "On the Beam," *Newsweek*, June 10, 1996, p. 81.
3. "Dominique Moceanu," *USA Gymnastics*, July/August 1995, p. 24.
4. Carolanne Griffith Roberts, "What it Takes to Raise a Winner," *Southern Living*, July 1996, p. 78.

Chapter 2 LEAVING

1. E.M. Swift, "Driving Dominique," *Sports Illustrated*, July 22, 1996, p. 90.
2. Kevin Sullivan, "Moceanu has World Whispering 'Nadia,' " *The Washington Post*, October 11, 1995, sec. F, p. 2.
3. Dominique Moceanu and Steve Woodward, Dominique Moceanu: An American Champion. Bantam Books: 1996, p. 23.

Chapter 3 BELA

1. Nancy Raymond, "Chatting with Jennie and Dominique," *International Gymnast*, March 1993, p. 12.
2. Skip Hollandsworth, "Bela Karolyi: I Have Made Their Lives Miserable," *Texas Monthly*, December 1991, p. 146.
3. Nancy Raymond, "Chatting with Jennie and Dominique," *International Gymnast*, March 1993, p. 12.
4. Bonnie DeSimone, "The Little Savior?" *The Chicago Tribune*, May 12, 1996, sec. 3, p. 5.
5. "Even at 13, a Storybook Career is Emerging," *The New York Times*, August 17, 1995, sec. B, p. 18.
6. Kevin Sullivan, "Moceanu has World Whispering 'Nadia,' " *The Washington Post*, October 11, 1995, sec. F, p. 2. This note applies to the immediately preceding quote as well.
7. Mark Starr, "Bounds for Glory," *Newsweek*, October 2, 1995, p. 73.
8. Bela Karolyi and Nancy Ann Richardson, Feel No Fear: The Power, Passion, & Politics of a Life in Gymnastics. Hyperion: 1994, p. 220.

186

9. Kevin Sullivan, "Moceanu has World Whispering 'Nadia,' " *The Washington Post*, October 11, 1995, sec. F, p. 2.

10. Joan Ryan, Little Girls in Pretty Boxes. Doubleday: 1995, pp. 242-243.

11. Mark McDonald, "A Grisly Pall Cast on Gymnastics," *The Star-Ledger*, August 20, 1995, sec. 5, p. 17.

12. Nancy Raymond, "Chatting with Jennie and Dominique," *International Gymnast*, March 1993, p. 12.

Chapter 4 BUILDING

1. Dominique Moceanu and Steve Woodward, Dominique Moceanu: An American Champion. Bantam Books: 1996, pp. 59-60.

2. Jill Smolowe, "Flexible Flyer," *Time*, Summer 1996, p. 65.

3. John P. Lopez, "Reason to Smile," *The Houston Chronicle*, January 28, 1996, sec. B, p. 1. This note applies to the immediately preceding quote as well.

Chapter 5 STEPPING INTO THE SPOTLIGHT

1. Heidi Pederson, "Exercising A Strong Will," *The New York Times*, February 4, 1996, sec. 8, p. 7. This note applies to the immediately preceding quote as well.

2. Dominique Moceanu and Steve Woodward, Dominique Moceanu: An American Champion. Bantam Books: 1996, p. 65.

3. "Dominique Moceanu," *USA Gymnastics*, July/August 1995, p. 24.

4. Dwight Normile, "We're Baaack," *International Gymnast*, April 1995, p. 11.

5. E.M. Swift, "Sports People," *Sport Illustrated*, May 8, 1995, p. 54.

6. Dwight Normile, "We're Baaack," *International Gymnast*, April 1995, p. 11.

7. Dominique Moceanu and Steve Woodward, Dominique Moceanu: An American Champion. Bantam Books: 1996, p. 32.

Chapter 6 SPARKLING

1. Luan Peszek, "Moceanu and Roethlisberger Make History," *USA*

Gymnastics, September/October 1995, p. 26.
2. "Even at 13, a Storybook Career is Emerging," *The New York Times*, August 17, 1995, sec. B, p. 18.
3. Jane Gottesman, "The Two Dominiques," *Women's Sports & Fitness*, February 1996, p. 29.

Chapter 7 NOTICED
1. John P. Lopez, "Older, Wiser Strug Back in Karolyi's Camp," *The Houston Chronicle*, January 6, 1996. This note applies to the immediately preceding quote as well.
2. Debbie Becker, "Strug Trains for Second Games," *USA Today*, March 1, 1996, sec. C, p. 6.
3. Debbie Becker, "USA's Top Gymnasts to Skip World Championships," *USA Today*, April 11, sec. C, p. 10.
4. Bernie Lincicome, "Next 'Darling' Not Girl-Next-Door Type," *The Chicago Tribune*, July 22, 1996, sec. 3, p. 1.
5. Jennifer Frey, "Moceanu Keeps Things in Balance," *The Washington Post*, June 4, 1996, sec. E, p. 7.
6. Vladimir Pisarev (translation by Elizabeth A. Squires), "Svetlana Boginskaya: 'We Have Lots of Cowboys in Texas,' " *Sovetsky Sport*, May 18, 1996, p. 4.
7. John P. Lopez, "Two Militiamen Arrested in Atlanta Bomb Plot," *The Houston Chronicle*, April 27, 1996, sec. A, p. 1. This note applies to the immediately preceding quote as well.
8. Jill Smolowe, "Flexible Flyer," *Time*, Summer 1996, pp. 68, 70.

Chapter 8 TRIALS AND TRIBULATIONS
1. Michael Knisley, "Nadia's Theme," *The Sporting News*, August 28, 1995, p. 5.
2. Heidi Pederson, "A New Name Tops U.S. Gymnastics," *The New York Times*, August 20, 1995, p. 11.
3. Richard O'Brien, "Lord Gym," *Sports Illustrated*, July 27, 1992, p. 52.
4. Kevin Sullivan, "Four Feet Five and Looming Large," *The Washington*

Notes

Post, October 11, 1995, sec. F, p. 1.
5. Mark Starr, "On the Beam," *Newsweek*, June 10, 1996, p. 81.
6. John P. Lopez, "Injury Threatens Moceanu's Hopes for '96 Olympics," *The Houston Chronicle*, June 18, 1996, sec. B, p. 1.
7. John P. Lopez, "Injury Threatens Moceanu's Hopes for '96 Olympics," *The Houston Chronicle*, June 18, 1996, sec. B, p. 1.
8. John P. Lopez, "Out of the Shadows," *The Houston Chronicle*, July 23, 1996.

Chapter 9 QUEST FOR GOLD

1. E.M. Swift, "Profile in Courage," *Sports Illustrated*, August 5, 1996, p. 61.

Chapter 10 FAME AND FORTUNE

1. "Alexander, Alexandra: Namesakes Ace Pre-Olympic Test in Atlanta," *International Gymnast*, January 1996, p. 9.
2. William Plummer and Laurel Brubaker Calkins, "Body Double," *People*, May 13, 1996, p. 82.
3. Fran Blinebury, "Golden Girls Meet Their Dreams," *The Houston Chronicle*, August 2, 1996, sec. B, p. 3. This note applies to the immediately preceding two quotes as well.
4. Tom Weir, "Tinkering with Rules has Tinkerbells Left Out," *USA Today*, July 23, 1996, sec. E, p. 8.
5. Jill Smolowe, "Flexible Flyer," *Time*, Summer 1996, p. 70.
6. Vahe Gregorian, "Best of Both: Is She Another Comaneci or Retton?" *The St. Louis Post-Dispatch*, June 9, 1996, sec. F, p. 3.
7. Gene Wojciechowski, "Compulsory Joy," *The Chicago Tribune*, July 22, 1996, sec. 3, p. 4.

EPILOGUE

1. Thomas Stinson, "The Prodigy," *The Atlanta Journal/Constitution*, July 14, 1996, p. 38.

FOR FURTHER READING:

The Magnificent Seven: The Authorized Story of American Gold
Written by Nancy H. Kleinbaum
Published by Bantam Books in 1996

Shannon Miller: America's Most Decorated Gymnast
Written by Krista Quiner
Published by The Bradford Book Company in 1996

Kim Zmeskal: Determination to Win
Written by Krista Quiner
Published by The Bradford Book Company in 1995

Women's Gymnastics: a history, Volume I
Written by Minot Simons II
Published by Welwyn Publishing Company in 1995

Feel No Fear: The Power, Passion, & Politics of a Life in Gymnastics
Written by Bela Karolyi and Nancy Ann Richardson
Published by Hyperion in 1994

FOR CHILDREN'S READING:

Dominique Moceanu: An American Champion
Written by Dominique Moceanu with Steve Woodward
Published by Bantam Books in 1996

Shannon Miller: Going for the Gold
Written by Septima Green
Published by Avon Books in 1996

ABOUT THE AUTHOR

Krista Quiner is an author of several gymnastics biographies. She grew up in Medina, Ohio, and currently resides in New Jersey with her husband. Formerly known as Krista Bailey, she was a competitive gymnast for fifteen years. She began her gymnastics career at Gymnastics World in Broadview Heights, Ohio. She competed as a class I gymnast at Gymnastics of Ohio in North Canton throughout high school and received a gymnastics scholarship to the University of Denver, an NCAA Division I school, where she set a school record on floor exercise. Krista holds a Bachelor's degree from the University of Denver in International Studies and French.